Simon King's
Wildguide

Simon King's Wildguide

A personal introduction
to the observation
and photography of
British wildlife

BBC BOOKS

Published by BBC Books,
a division of BBC Enterprises Limited,
Woodlands, 80 Wood Lane
London W12 0TT

First published 1994
© Simon King 1994
ISBN 0 563 36496 3

Designed by Harry Green
Illustrations by John Busby
Photographs by Simon King except badger photograph
between pages 64 and 65 by Michael Leach (BBC Copyright)

Set in Bembo by Selwood Systems,
Midsomer Norton
Printed and bound in Great Britain
by Butler & Tanner Ltd, Frome and London
Colour separation by Technik Ltd, Berkhamsted.
Jacket printed by Lawrence Allen Ltd,
Weston-super-Mare

For Kim,

whose care

and understanding

during my long

absences watching

wildlife have

made this book

possible

Contents

Introduction

The natural world provides all manner of mysteries and puzzles to be unravelled. When you first develop an interest, the greatest challenge is undoubtedly identifying all that you see, but as you spend more time outdoors in search of wild animals, you begin to develop a skill which may take many years to perfect, that of field craft.

What is field craft? It is the ability to see when others are blind, to hear when others are deaf, to predict the unexpected and to behave appropriately in the most challenging of circumstances. It is something that is normally acquired by trial and error, and this book is an attempt to make the process a little easier, both for you and the animals you are trying to watch.

I have tried to cover the subjects and species in Britain which I am most often asked about, and this priority has also dictated the order in which I have presented the mammal species. According to accepted taxonomic order, voles come before otters, but I certainly receive more enquiries regarding otter watching than I do vole watching. I have dealt with the birds a little differently, sticking more closely to the generally accepted order of species.

This is a very personal guide, with much anecdotal evidence rather than hard fact, though everything I have written about has worked well for me.

Throughout the book I have described practical methods which should enhance your wildlife watching, but there is an equally important element to successful watching which is extremely difficult to pin down. Without wishing to sound mawkish, it involves the use of your heart. It is only with your heart that you will begin to understand all that you see. Your heart can tell you when something is about to happen, when you should and should not move, when you are accepted and when you are causing a disturbance. If you do not listen to your heart you will never be truly close to the wild, because it is only with a genuine regard—a love, if you will—of wild things that you will be able to feel at one with them.

SIMON KING

Section 1

Look Hear!

Using Your Eyes

The single most important factor in becoming a successful field naturalist is being able to see properly. By this, I do not mean having twenty-twenty vision, though this undoubtedly helps, but the ability to use your eyes to their full potential. Most people who are new to watching wildlife find that the number of creatures they can spot is limited. This is never more apparent than when walking with somebody who has more experience in the field.

I can clearly remember my first impressions whilst out with Michael Kendal, the man who was to become my friend and mentor, both on and off screen, in the television series *Man and Boy*. Mike, who has a fantastic knowledge of wild things, particularly British birds, would invite me to accompany him on bird watching trips. Together we would visit reservoirs, estuaries and woodlands, and in each, Mike would exclaim 'Look' and 'Shh!' as he spotted seemingly invisible birds and other animals. Here was a man who could pick out a little owl, hidden amongst a tangle of willow branches, or spot a sparrowhawk virtually before it came into view. He could do the impossible and it made me feel at once thrilled and frustrated: thrilled that I too might eventually be able to achieve this level of awareness; frustrated that for years I had been ferreting about in woodland, only seeing a fraction of what was around me. I was always looking but I couldn't see.

Trying to analyse the enormous difference between looking and seeing is almost as challenging as making the transition between the two. Everybody *looks* whilst they are in the countryside. They look at the view, the sky, their feet, in fact anything that falls into their direct field of vision. And here, I believe, lies the most fundamental problem which prevents us from seeing well. We all of us start out with a very blinkered view of the world and this is hardly surprising. As we leave the safety of our homes, very few of us have to hunt for our next meal. Neither do we have to keep a constant eye out for danger. In our twentieth-century existence we have lost the survivor's edge. In order to see well, there must be more than a desire to do so: there must be a need. Most wild creatures feel this need, for them it can make the difference between life and death. Indeed, it is their acute sense of awareness that makes it difficult for us to see them.

But you can hone this ability by adopting a few simple techniques. Be aware of the slightest sound, the smallest movement. Develop peripheral vision. By responding immediately to movement seen in the corner of your eye, you increase your chances of spotting an animal ten-fold. The feeling one has sometimes of being watched can be explained, in part, by this underused element of eyesight. Frequently, a movement or irregular shape just on the edge of your view stops you in your tracks and makes your hackles rise without you realizing quite why.

Make a point of moving your head more. By this I mean left, right, up and down. It may sound obvious to say that by scanning your field of view over a greater area you cover more ground and see more, but it's easy to walk with your eyes locked on what lies straight ahead or just in front of your feet without thinking. By constantly scanning, you increase your chances of seeing not only the animals themselves but also their tracks and signs.

Knowing where to look for animals also makes a huge difference to how many you will see. There are certain features that are always worth closer scrutiny. Fence posts and telegraph poles are classic examples. Owls and birds of prey in particular use these as look-out stations from which to hunt. Usually these birds are well camouflaged, their cryptic plumage matching the browns and greys of the post on which they are perched. A closer look can often reveal that the odd bump on top of the post is in fact alive.

Certain other features warrant a second glance. Anything that shows up pale or dark against the general background is worth another look. Despite superb camouflage, under the right conditions, a great many animals can be highly visible over large distances. The russet hue of a roe deer in summer can be seen from at least half a kilometre away, especially if it is grazing in pasture-land. The dark, hunched form of a kestrel perched on an overhead wire is equally noticeable. The basic rule is to take note of the unusual, however small the detail, and to remain constantly alert. After a while, this attitude will become second nature, and you may begin to wonder how you ever behaved otherwise.

If you regularly walk in a favourite spot, it pays to familiarize yourself with every branch, every post, every rocky outcrop. The better you know the look of an area, the more chance you have of spying the unusual. This seems to be especially true if you are trying to find one particular type of animal. Whilst looking for hares, I have often been fooled into thinking that a distant tuft of brown grass is an animal. By making a mental note of its whereabouts, I have been able to disregard the grass the next time round, and concentrate instead on looking for the real thing. Similarly, oddly shaped branches, stones and a multitude of other forms can mislead you for a time. Like a wild animal, the better you know your home ground, the more chance you have of success.

A word or two about seeing things under adverse conditions. Perhaps the most difficult of these to deal with is darkness.

It is dusk. You have spent the past two hours sitting motionless, waiting for a badger to emerge from its sett, but to no avail. The light is fading fast, only the faintest glow still hangs in the West. Just as you are contemplating getting up to leave, there is a rustle from the undergrowth ahead of you. You freeze, strain your eyes in the direction of the sound, but can see nothing. This is the moment when you need to use your peripheral vision.

The human eye is well endowed with light-sensitive cells which react to colour, but it is poorly developed for seeing in low-light conditions. The portion of our retina which contains most of the cells that respond to colourless light is just off centre. By looking to the side of an object, and concentrating on the peripheral view, you are far more likely to see movement and form than by staring straight at it.

A sure way to ruin your night vision is to use any form of artificial light. Just as walking into a dark room having been exposed to bright light initially renders you blind, so using a torch temporarily dulls your ability to see in the shadows.

Bright light can sometimes prove to be almost as difficult for spotting animals as no light. True, this is something encountered more in equatorial regions than duller northern climes, but nonetheless, it can prove to be a real problem anywhere in the world. Some naturalists regularly wear good quality sun-glasses and continue to spot well. Wearing glasses can alleviate the constant strain of squinting, which often leads to headaches, and at the same time protect the eyes against the sun's harmful ultraviolet rays. Many sun-glasses, however, are tinted with a colour, often sepia or even pink. This colour may enhance the view for some people, but it certainly does nothing to help you spot animals. The frames also cut down the field of view, which, as already stated, is an important element in picking out movement and form.

Carefully chosen glasses can provide a positive advantage under certain circumstances. Colourless, neutral-density lenses, with polarizing filters, can make searching across hot, hazy, open ground a good deal easier on the eye. They can also help in watery habitats where there is a lot of glare and polarized light about. Bleary eyes caused by wind can be very irritating and glasses of any description can also help in very breezy conditions, particularly if you have to face into a gale as so often happens in coastal habitats.

None of these techniques will help you to identify creatures, only pick them out in the first place. The interim period of frustration, as you begin to see more and more yet feel you know less and less, can be a stumbling block for many who set out to learn about wild animals. My only advice here is to persevere, struggle with the field guides, listen to the recordings of birdsong, and bit by bit the enormous variety and colour of the natural world will begin to unfold before you.

Using Your Ears

The second most important sense for the field naturalist is hearing. Many creatures betray their presence by making a sound, either directly or indirectly. The direct sounds come in the form of any vocalization or intentional audible message sent out by the animal; the indirect sounds come from vegetation being disturbed or the effect an animal has on its neighbours. The latter is particularly important for spotting predators.

There is not a lot you can do to enhance your hearing other than practise. So much of being able to understand natural sounds depends on being able to identify them in the first place, and that can feel very daunting at first. With time the subtleties of tone and pitch start to separate the species, and the great morass of natural sound you first experience begins to separate into individual calls and rustles, and, just as you can learn to identify the voice of a friend or relative, so you can learn the language of the wild. Once you are able to identify a few vocalizations, learning new ones becomes much easier.

I believe that most of us are capable of picking up much smaller sounds than perhaps we know. We are all familiar with that feeling when, in the middle of the night, we are woken by a noise somewhere in the house. In the small hours, every tiny sound seems to echo and reverberate. Fear has an important part to play in hearing well. Wild animals use their ears all the time to pin-point danger, and it is this sort of acuity you want to nurture when watching wildlife. Strain to listen the whole time, and you will hear a great deal more.

Animal voices can obviously tell you a lot about the species making them, but other sounds can be equally helpful. Many creatures move in unique ways and this often betrays not only their whereabouts but also what they are.

Predatory species, whether birds or mammals, spend a great deal of their lives being harried by the creatures who may feature in their diet. Mobbing behaviour, as it's known, is a way in which vulnerable animals keep a check on their foe and alert others of the danger. And the others include us. I spot a large percentage of the hunting species by responding to the alarm calls of small birds and some mammals. Some of these calls are so specific that you can guess the nature of the danger just by hearing them, and so direct the search in the right area.

There are one or two practical methods for enhancing your hearing sensitivity and accuracy. For example, cupping your hands behind your ears *can* make a difference to hearing better. This is particularly true under certain conditions. Some sounds, though quite loud, are terribly difficult to locate. A fine example is the song of the grasshopper warbler, whose rattling trill apparently comes and goes on the breeze from nowhere in particular. I have spent many frustrating minutes searching for the little bird, only to find that I have been scouring the wrong thicket as it pops up somewhere to my left or right. A good way of establishing the source of a sound is to use your hands, cupped quite close to the ears, and slowly pan your head through a horizontal plane. Make a mental note of when the sound is at its loudest, then repeat the process. Repetition is important because animals, like the grasshopper warbler, are constantly turning this way and that, resulting in a rise and fall in volume.

Many insects, especially the grasshoppers and crickets, have a similar quality of 'voice' to the grasshopper warbler, and can be equally tricky to locate. A similar method using cupped hands is helpful, though it's as well to remember that the insects are rarely as distant as you think.

Using your hands as sonic reflectors works just as well in reverse. This is particularly useful if you are trying to keep movement of your head to a minimum, essential when watching creatures with good eyesight. Should such a creature decide to walk behind you, it is possible to keep tabs on it simply by cupping your hands in front of your ears and listening to its progress.

But there are far more technical enhancers to hearing than the human hand, some of which are very useful for certain forms of wildlife watching. The best known of these is the bat detector. These little magic boxes convert ultrasonic calls into electronic clicks. This conversion not only allows us to 'hear' the bat, but on many occasions to identify its species. Each type of bat emits squeaks at a distinctive rate and pitch, which the detector can be adjusted to receive, thus revealing the frequency range the animal is using. Getting hold of these detectors is quite straightforward, though not exactly cheap. Several electronics companies produce them and advertise through specialist magazines and journals. Many counties in Britain have bat groups, usually affiliated to local conservation trusts, and these will also help provide information on the best type of detectors and where to get one.

Another form of audio enhancement is the parabolic reflector. This does the same job as your hands, only better. It narrows the range of a microphone so that it picks up only the sound it is pointing at. This equipment can be used with headphones alone but is more normally used in conjunction with a recording device of some sort.

There is also a bewildering array of microphones which can pick up sounds over some distance. Generally referred to as 'gun mikes', these tend to provide a more natural-sounding recording but inevitably include more extraneous noises than the reflector. DAT (digital audio tape) can reproduce sound accurately without the problem of tape hiss, and this will enhance the quality of your recording.

Wildlife sound-recording can be an extremely rewarding hobby, which not only provides an enduring record of your experiences but can help a great deal with identifying birdsong and other natural sounds. A successful recording of an animal is every bit as rewarding as a good photograph of the same.

A Moving Experience

Whatever your intentions, all people are regarded with varying degrees of fear by most animals. This is the naturalist's greatest handicap, and the reason for the myriad ploys developed for avoiding detection. One of the things you learn as you spend more and more time out in the wilds in search of animals, is how to move without disturbing them too much.

The first thing to think about is whether you should move at all. You can get much better views of some animals if you work out where they are likely to be and get there first. The golden rule whilst waiting for such an event is to behave as though you are being watched the whole time; sooner or later you'll be right. This means that as well as keeping quiet, any move you do make, however slight, must be done slowly. The most common mistake I made when first learning how to move effectively, was turning my head too rapidly when I thought I had spotted something from the corner of my eye. This had the inevitable effect of startling the creature into fright or flight. Every move must be considered, careful, deliberate. If you watch a roe deer walking through a woodland, you will notice that almost every step is taken as though the animal were walking on hot coals. With every pause it senses the wind and looks fearfully about it. To get good views of an animal like this, you must beat it at its own game.

As bi-ped mammals, we are at something of a disadvantage when it comes to walking quietly. A four-legged beast can stop, mid-stride, at any point of its progress. We, on the other hand, must fall on to each foot in order to go forward. This is a pretty noisy way of moving around, and to counteract the effect, we must concentrate hard on controlling the noise level. This can be very difficult in woodland, where dead leaves and twigs can produce earth-shattering sound, but I have found that in all habitats there are ways of reducing noise from the feet. When walking, I maintain constant tension in my legs, slightly bending my knees the whole time. In this manner I have far more control over my weight distribution than if I allowed myself to walk in a more relaxed manner. If a twig starts to creak underfoot, I can shift my step to avoid breaking it; in a normal walk I would be committed to the step and the resulting noise. I also use a deliberate 'heel-toe' action which helps to distribute my weight slowly and evenly over the ground.

As well as being noisy, we stink. We can't help it, but judging by the reaction of most wild mammals to human scent, we stink a lot! The only way you can counteract this is to be constantly aware of wind direction. There are many traditional ways of doing this. The simplest and best known method is to wet your finger in your mouth, hold it in the air and discern which side gets cold first. This does not work too well, however, if you already have cold hands or if you are wearing gloves. Seriously though, the wet-finger method is inaccurate at the best of times. A much more accurate method is to release some light object, such as a blade of grass or dead leaf into the breeze, and watch its progress. This can be especially valuable if the wind is eddying or changeable, though it can be surprisingly hard to find an object light enough to drift on a gentle breeze when you need one. Some people carry around a small bag of pepper or similar substance for this purpose. At certain times of year, natural wind gauges like dandelion seeds are plentiful, but failing this I sometimes use dry soil, crumbled into a fine powder, or tree bark flaked between finger and thumb.

With a bit of practise, you can sense even the gentlest breath of air on your face and neck and so keep a running check on wind direction. I believe that one of the strongest human scents is our own breath. And no, I'm not the sort of person who sucks mints all day. Some ground-nesting birds, such as grouse, slow their breathing rate as danger approaches, almost to the point of holding it completely. Then, when the danger gets too close, they suddenly increase their breathing and heart rates as they burst into flight. It seems fair to assume that this behaviour has developed because many mammalian predators home in on the smell of their quarry's breath more than any other scent. When an animal is unavoidably about to pass downwind of me, I usually try to breathe very shallowly, or hold my breath altogether. There are many occasions when this has made no difference whatsoever, but there have been times when the animal has failed to detect my presence. Whether or not this method works, it certainly adds to the sense of excitement and expectation during a watch.

The Art of Invisibility

You can't move around or wait undetected without successful camouflage. Obvious as it may seem, you must pick your camouflage to suit your surroundings, and this doesn't always mean a green and black 'cammo' jacket. Think about where you are going to be watching wildlife and choose the colours of your clothes accordingly.

If you have dark skin you are at a distinct advantage, because the flash of a white hand or face shows up like a beacon in most habitats. There are several ways of disguising this. In summer, I use green and brown face paint, available from most army surplus stores. Look at well camouflaged animals for clues on how best to use the paint.

Many moths, woodcock, nightjar and others all have a muddled blend of browns, blacks and perhaps surprisingly, white, in their colour schemes. The pale areas help disrupt the outline of the animal, catching the eye without revealing the form, just like sunlight reflecting on undergrowth. Using the same strategy, it is a good idea to leave a few bits of skin clear of paint, particularly for camouflage during the day. Similarly if your skin is dark, then some pale green or buff-coloured stripes will help to break up your outline.

On occasions when I have been caught short without any face paint, I have always found mud to be a good substitute. The contents of a mucky puddle, sloshed on to the hands and face help you blend immediately into your surroundings. (It pays to clean the palms of your hands before handling cameras.) The problems only arise when you pop into the corner shop for a pint of milk on the way home, as has happened to me on several occasions, when I have been greeted with a mixture of fear and pity.

If you're not keen on daubing muck all over yourself, then there are lightweight camouflaged gloves and face nets available from army surplus stores. They work well, but the face nets can impair vision, and the gloves can make it fiddly to handle delicate camera gear. In cold weather, a dark balaclava and gloves are both warm and practical for covering pale skin. I have used woollen shooting-style gloves for many years and find that the exposed index finger of the right hand can deal with most operations needed on a stills or cine camera. Many people swear by a peaked hat or cap in all weathers, the peak casting their face into shadow and so toning it down. Though effective for this purpose, I find that any peak above my eyes cuts out a valuable line of sight to the sky and tree canopy.

Of all the parts of the human body, our head is the one that seems to distinguish us instantly to other animals. I therefore often take the trouble to make the outline of my head as irregular as possible. I do not achieve this by running into brick walls head first. What I do use is a sort of netting hat into which I stick all manner of vegetation—bracken is ideal, dead and brown, or alive and green, according to the time of year. It is worth taking the time to secure carefully each frond in place, or else you may end up with a leaf tickling your nose or dropping in front of your eyes at the wrong moment.

Hide and Seek

If you do not intend moving around to watch animals, then you can consider using a hide. There are not many ready-made models available, and most that are serve a purpose, but have some problems associated with them. The first is the frame. One popular design comes with four poles and guy ropes to support the canvas. Trying to secure these on a pebbly beach during a gale constitutes a challenge of the greatest magnitude. A hide frame should have at least four cross-bars across the top, and be able to stand without extra support before you even think about trying to pull the canvas over. There is a wonderful clamp which is ideally suited to this task, available from shop-fitters. More normally used to hold metal bars together in clothing displays, these three-way rod clamps are great for securing lengths of wooden dowel, or broom handles into a perfect, square hide frame. A more refined structure may include a couple of rods across the inside of the roof, which will prevent rain building up and creating a worrying sag above your head. I have made and have had made many different designs of frame and have settled on a lightweight alloy construction which folds away very neatly and seems to absorb most bumps and bangs when erected.

The design of the canvas is a very personal choice, depending on whether you wish to use the hide for stills photography, cine, observation, or all three. The traditional camera funnel (a sleeve of canvas, elasticized at one end to fit snugly around the lens) is, I think, of limited practical use. It has two major flaws. The first is that if wind starts to move the hide canvas, then the lens poking through the funnel is also affected. Whether you are taking stills photographs or moving images, stability is of paramount importance to the results.

The second problem with the design is lack of view. Even if you are photographing a nesting bird, it is essential that you are able to see some of the area around the centre of interest. You can then spot the unusual before it happens—perhaps the other adult arriving or a predator skulking nearby. Even with a small observation window cut out above the funnel, each time you put your eye to the camera you lose sight of everything apart from that which you can see through the viewfinder. The one great advantage of a camera funnel is that your subject can see nothing but the camera lens. There is, however, a method by which you can have a large observation and lens window and still prevent your own movements from being seen.

My own hides have windows measuring the whole width of the front and about 40 cm in depth. Such a large window runs the risk of exposing every move I make, so to ensure this doesn't happen, I hang green netting across the opening. This works on the same principle as a net curtain. A hide should be made of canvas or other fabric that is virtually light-proof. This not only ensures that your silhouette doesn't show through, but also provides a very dark interior, essential for large observation ports. Light shining on the netting catches the eye (and closes the pupil) to such an extent that the dark interior is rendered invisible. Very few diurnal (those active in daylight hours) animals can see past the netting, but I am able to see them quite clearly. Even when one eye is on the camera, my other eye can be open and scanning for any other movement nearby. It is important that only one window is used at a time, otherwise you run the risk of your outline showing.

The introduction of a hide into a habitat can be quite disruptive if not done properly. Each species must be approached according to its senses and reaction to change. Generally, it is not enough to assume the hide in itself is sufficient to put your subject at ease, and you will often have to hide the hide. By carefully blending it into the surrounding habitat, you stand a far greater chance of successful observation and are much less likely to cause disturbance. Even if the species you are working with is happy to tolerate the basic canvas structure, other people may see the hide and, by investigating, unwittingly disturb the site. I have also lost several hides to vandalism. All the portable hides I have made for me, now, include a second skin of netting. I find this ideal for tying in vegetation from the surrounding habitat. Spend a bit of time and care doing this; if you can still see the structure, so will everyone else.

There are some habitats, such as open fields or mud flats, where complete disguise is impossible. I once set up a hide to film roosting waders on a muddy beach on the Wirral. In an attempt to keep the whole thing inconspicuous, I shortened the legs to no more than half a metre, as low as I could go, and still be able to fit myself and the camera inside. Having carefully tied rushes and other coastal plants to the sides, I clambered in before the tide started to rise, bringing the birds to within filming distance. The following three and a half hours were not the most comfortable I have spent in my life, as the rising water slowly saturated the mud I was lying in, and my legs went from having pins and needles, to cramp, to just plain numb. Slowly though, my plan was working. I could see a huge flock of knot and dunlin being nudged up the shoreline by the rising water. Within half an hour they would be all around me, providing superb low-level images. Just then, a voice rang out: 'I wonder if anyone is inside?' The flock of waders scattered as the lady walking her dog moved around to the front of the hide to investigate its contents. I'm afraid my gruff response may have unnerved her a little.

Other features on my hides include large pockets underneath each window. These hold everything from spare film to flasks of tea; stone pockets around the bottom to weigh the whole thing down; ribbon ties to hold the back flap in place, and which provide a near noiseless exit and window covers, fixed by Velcro. I have tried other ways of fixing the window covers, including popper studs and zips, but despite the disadvantage of noise, still find Velcro to be the most adaptable and effective.

There are two main ways of using a hide: one is to set it up and try to attract animals within sight; the other is carefully to introduce it to a location to which you know the animal is likely to return. The first of these stands the least chance of causing any disturbance, as the animal is at liberty to avoid you if it feels so inclined. The second can be very risky if not undertaken responsibly. This is especially true where nesting birds are concerned, because the slightest disturbance can cause them to abandon their eggs or young. Every species is different and must be treated accordingly.

If you set up a hide in a field containing livestock, then be aware that you are likely to become the centre of attention. Whilst filming a skylark nest, I was once harassed by a couple of horses who were grazing in the same pasture. One in particular spent most of its time hanging around the hide, from time to time sticking his great snout down on to the canvas roof, and sliding it backwards and forwards. He was a little startled when I tried to push him away from within. The biggest problem was that his feet threatened to crush the nest which was only yards away. The remedy was an electric fence hastily erected around the site.

To reduce further the risk of disturbing the animal you want to observe, you will often need the services of a walk-away. The method works on the understanding that the animal you are watching can't count, a principle which is not always true. A walk-away is a sort of decoy, somebody who accompanies you to the hide and then leaves once you are comfortably ensconced. The same person can then approach the hide and retrieve you at the end of the day. Both actions are designed to convince your subject that human beings only visit the hide for short periods and never remain within.

Often the biggest problem is finding a person who is prepared to take on the task, because it not only entails hours spent waiting, perhaps in a car or behind a hedge, but waiting in the certain knowledge that your colleague in the hide is getting stunning views of an animal that you can only see as a speck at best.

I have been very lucky, but I was once left in the lurch whilst working with a buzzard's nest in Somerset. The hide was built on top of a 14 metre scaffolding tower, 9 metres from the nest. I had been filming the female buzzard while she fed and incubated her chicks for the best part of ten hours, and felt satisfied with the day's work when the prearranged time came to leave. The feeling evaporated as ten minutes, then twenty, then fifty elapsed with no sign of my assistant. As the sky began to darken I decided I would have to leave the hide, or risk disturbing the parent bird at night when the darkness might have prevented her from returning to her chicks. The problem was how to do so without making her fearful of the hide thereafter. I decided that as it was people she was afraid of, I would have to make myself look as inhuman as possible. Pulling my shirt over my head and generally re-arranging all my other clothes, I slowly began to exit from the rear of the hide. To add to the effect, I chose to make the descent upside down. I was later to discover that the reason behind the absence of the walk-away had something to do with extended TV coverage of play at Lords. In fact, the necessity for a walk-away varies greatly according to the species and sometimes the individual animal you are working with. As a general rule, the smaller perching birds seem unperturbed by the comings and goings of a lone human, whereas larger species, especially the crow family, wading birds and birds of prey are much more sensitive.

Under certain conditions, it is possible to enter and exit from a hide by putting the structure between yourself and your subject, crawling quietly and carefully into position unobserved. If you use this method as a way of retreating, then once you have managed to scrabble a fair distance unseen, it is a good idea to make a little noise before popping up into full view. This gives your subject a chance to suspect some-one is coming rather than surprising it by appearing out of thin air. There are, of course, no golden rules, barring that of the animal's welfare being your most important consideration, and at the first sign of disturbance you must abandon your activities before your subjects abandon theirs.

A portable canvas hide is not the only means of disguising your outline while animal watching. There are circumstances when a more open screen is ideal for the job and I often use a section or sections of scrim for the purpose. Scrim is the netting used by the armed forces to camouflage equipment and personnel, and varies from small sheets of the close weave variety (good for hanging in hide windows) to the much larger open weave that is traditionally used for concealing tanks and artillery. The latter is an excellent basis for building an observation screen. Strung between existing vegetation and augmented with fronds of local greenery, it can provide a quick and easy camouflage for watching a variety of animals. It is always important to choose the site for such a screen carefully. It should benefit from natural shading and dense vegetation to the sides, and, more importantly, directly behind. Much the same effect can be achieved without a scrim using only available sticks and leaves, but it takes a great deal longer to set up. This sort of 'natural' hide is sometimes your only option if caught short in the field without any other form of concealment. I have used everything from a hole in the ground to a pile of rocks, all to great effect.

Once safely installed into whichever type of hide you have chosen to use, there are a few points worth considering. Don't make yourself too comfortable: it can be terribly frustrating or even dangerous. I learnt this lesson the first time I ever filmed a sparrowhawk nest from a tower hide. The seat I chose to use, though of the folding variety, had arm rests and a high back. For the first few days I remained alert, spurred on by such intimate and privileged views of this dashing and restless bird. Raptors, such as sparrowhawks, however, can leave quite long periods between visits to the nest, particularly once the chicks have grown a bit. By the fourth day of filming, some of the novelty of watching the chicks snoozing between feeds had worn off and I was beginning to feel the effects of consecutive sessions lasting thirteen hours each in the hide. The warm sun heated the roof, flies buzzed around the nest, the chicks sagged into a white ball of sleep. Suddenly the adult female arrived on the edge with the remains of a thrush clenched in her talons and began to feed her clamorous offspring. I tried gently easing forward to train the camera on the action but found myself paralysed, unable to respond to this moment of drama. This was a nightmare. This WAS a nightmare! I came round in a fit of panic and confusion to see an immobile heap of sleepy chicks. Absolutely nothing had happened apart from my dozing off in the warm embrace of a comfy chair, or at least I didn't think so.

The trouble was I could not be certain what, if anything, I had missed. Since that experience I have used only the flimsiest of folding stools which require a degree of conscious effort to remain seated on. Now if I doze off, I fall off, and can be certain I've missed nothing.

The amount of time you are likely to spend in the hide necessitates a degree of planning for the day ahead. Food and drink are important, so, too, is a means of relieving yourself. It is horribly annoying to find that nature calls just as Nature outside is getting interesting.

If you plan to use any form of camera, then it is important to acclimatize your subject to the lens. I do this by leaving a dummy lens hanging in the hide window once the structure has been accepted and before I have started filming. How accurately this dummy should replicate a real lens can differ depending on the animal you wish to photograph, but it is worth playing safe and making something that would fool most people if seen at a glance. Bottles, plastic or glass, are a good basis for most dummy lenses, because it is the reflective surface of the lens which some animals find unsettling at first.

Equipment

BINS & SCOPES

Only one piece of equipment is absolutely essential for the field naturalist: a pair of binoculars or bins for short. Given their importance, it is worth spending a bit of time considering the sort best suited to your needs and then spending as much on them as you feel you can afford. As a general rule, the greater the cost, the higher the quality of workmanship and reliability.

Binoculars are described with two numbers: the first indicates the magnification; the second reveals the diameter of the objective lens. In a pair of 7×42 binoculars, you have an image which appears seven times larger than that seen with the naked eye, and an objective lens measuring 42 mm across. A bigger lens lets in more light, though the magnification also has to be taken into account when working out how bright the image will be.

The range of magnifications that are practical for wildlife watching is fairly narrow, between 7 × and 10 ×. Any more than this is very difficult to hold stable without a tripod, and even 10 × can be pretty wobbly unless you support your elbows whilst viewing. There are some highly specialized bins, which despite high magnification manage a fairly stable image with a remarkable system of 'floating' lenses, held in suspension by magnets. These are very large and heavy and ill suited to general field use.

When deciding which type of binoculars to buy, you need to consider several factors. Do you want them to fit into a pocket? Do they have to be waterproof? Are you using them to watch birds, mammals, insects or all three?

Let's start with size. Very small binoculars are light, can be stored in a pocket or briefcase, are easy for children to use and are usually less expensive than their bigger cousins. But they do not work well in low light, their definition is often poor and their construction relatively flimsy. Compact binoculars (usually any with an objective lens of less than 30 mm) are often used by people as a 'go-anywhere-pair' in addition to a pair used when actively watching wildlife.

There are two main types of larger designs, the roof-prism and the poro-prism. Roof-prism are usually regarded as being built to the highest specification, their greatest advantage being that they are relatively small and easy to hold, while at the same time offering first-class optics. Poro-prism binoculars are the traditional style which, though not quite as user-friendly as the roof-prism variety, can offer excellent value for money. If you are serious about watching animals, then you should choose from one of these two types of larger binoculars.

Next, you should consider what kind of animal you are likely to be looking for. Most European mammals are crepuscular or nocturnal: (they spend most of the day sleeping and only become truly active around dusk and dawn or throughout the night). The most important feature to look for in binoculars for mammal watching is therefore good performance in low light. The wider the objective lens, the more light is able to enter the optics, so anything less than a lens measuring 30 mm isn't really worth considering. Bins with huge objective lenses, however, can be very heavy and unwieldy. My first pair of binoculars were an inherited pair of 10 × 50s, produced by a well known high-street chemist. These enormous bottles made me feel very professional (at the age of eight) and so it was with the greatest reluctance that I would admit to anyone that they not only gave me terrible neck ache but also that I could barely see a thing through them. The combination of weight, size, magnification and misalignment resulted in what was probably a budding naturalist's worst enemy.

Mammal watching can involve a lot of scrabbling about on your hands and knees to avoid being seen, so your binoculars will have to be of a size that can easily be stowed inside a jacket or behind your back. Failure to do this can result in a black eye, but not from bruising. The exposed eye cups are wonderfully adept at collecting wet mud, and are just as good at dumping their filthy contents into an unsuspecting eye socket.

Unlike mammals, watching birds does not usually depend so much on seeing well in bad light, but rather requires close views of little creatures which are often set against a bright sky. Some binoculars (such as my old 10 × 50s) do all sorts of strange things when you use them against the light. I once tried to watch a pair of nesting sparrowhawks in my local woodland, which had chosen the top of a tall Scots pine to raise their brood. Each time the dark form of the female arrived to feed the chicks, I would raise my bins, only to be blinded by a cloud of flare and shattered colour resulting from the brilliance of the pale sky. Most binoculars now have special coatings on their lenses which help prevent this sort of optical disaster, and naturally, some makes and models are better at it than others.

Insect and reptile watching requires binoculars that can focus to within a few feet of the observer. This is a feature which is quite hard to include in the mechanics of most binocular designs, and by and large is something that you have to pay for. It can be terribly frustrating if you spot a dragonfly you think may be a rarity only to find your bins just can't focus down to the short distance. You then face the dilemma of whether or not to step backwards into the range of minimum focus or else to try stalking forward close enough to see detail with the naked eye. By the time you've made up your mind, your quarry has invariably flown off.

Whatever type of animal you plan to watch, there is undoubtedly a pair of binoculars to suit it. The best makes are practical for any kind of application but if you are on a tight budget then test before you buy, bearing in mind what you need from the equipment.

Unless you plan to use your bins on the sea or from a boat regularly, then the protection afforded by waterproof binoculars is not strictly necessary. The chances are that if you do drop them in deep water you'll never see them again anyway, so it's little comfort to know that they're not leaking. Rubber coating does not make binoculars waterproof, but it does protect them against the knocks they will incur in field use. True, the rubber does make them a bit heavier, but having 'knocked' my own binoculars very hard in the past, I am now a firm advocate of the armoured variety.

On the subject of rubber, if you wear glasses, then you will need rubber eye cups on your bins, which, folded back, allow a reasonable field of view with your glasses still on. Equally, if you do not wear glasses and, like me, prefer a firm eye cup, it may be worth checking whether this is a feature which can be changed.

Most bins come complete with a lanyard or strap, but in my opinion too little thought is given to this important part of the equipment. An uncomfortable strap can chafe the back of the neck, particularly in summer, when you're less likely to be sporting a high collar for protection. There are a great many camera straps available on the market, some of which do very well for binoculars, and which are much more comfy than the spindly things that come with many bins.

Another added extra that, once you've tried it out, becomes an essential piece of kit is a rain-guard. This simple hood slides down the lanyard and covers the eye pieces when the bins are not in use. The advantages of using this device are not restricted to keeping the rain off. Many is the time I've brought my bins up to my eyes only to be blinded by dust and grit. This is especially likely to happen in woodland where every tree and bush you brush against dumps its quota of muck into the eye cups. If your chosen brand of binoculars doesn't come with a rain-guard, get one or make one; it will save you a lot of grief.

Using binoculars properly comes naturally to many people, though often not before they have missed many opportunities while practising. Most new bins come with instructions on how to set the adjustable eyepiece correctly. Some also describe how to set the lenses for the proper distance between your eyes; you should end up with a view that appears more or less circular and not the double, joined circles so beloved of Hollywood films. But the most common problem occurs when trying to get a fix on a small subject, set against a background which has few or no distinctive features. I can well recall the struggle to find a wood warbler high up in the leaf canopy or a distant peregrine falcon in a cloudless sky. The problem with lining up binoculars quickly and accurately on a subject can, however, be very easily overcome. Having spotted an animal, keep your gaze fixed on it, then, without looking down, take your binoculars in hand and slowly bring them up to your eyes. It is essential that your gaze does not waver from the direction of your intended view for an instant, not even as the binocular casing comes in front of your eyes, momentarily blinding you. By adjusting the position of the binoculars so that the lenses coincide with your line of sight, you ensure rapid and accurate location every time.

Now and again the animal you are trying to see is just too far away for the limited magnification of most binoculars. Some people use zoom binoculars for this purpose, but the best tool for the job is undoubtedly a telescope. Many of the practical criteria which apply to binoculars also apply to scopes, but before you rush out to get one it's worth considering a couple of factors.

First, do you really need one? It is easy to assume that a telescope is a necessary piece of equipment for all field naturalists, but in truth there are very few occasions when the use of one is absolutely essential. If you expect to be searching across great distances for animals, perhaps on an estuary or a large lake, then a scope can make the difference between properly identifying a species or not. This applies especially to bird watchers trying to tell the difference between, let's say, a dunlin and a curlew sandpiper, on a distant mud flat. The use of a telescope is also particularly suited when studying deer in wide open country such as the highlands of Scotland. But if you expect to spend most of your time animal watching in woodland or other enclosed habitats, then it will be of little use to you.

Second, do you want to carry the extra weight? Most telescopes are quite bulky and they invariably need a tripod to steady them. The combined weight can be considerable and quite inconvenient to carry.

Telescopes come in two main varieties: the original and truly tele-scopic models as used by swash-buckling pirates, etc, and the more modern fixed-body design. The 'telescopic' designs have the advantage of squeezing down into a compact unit, but they are slightly unwieldy when fully extended. The fixed-body models are either quite chunky to allow for the necessary distance between the objective lens and the eyepiece, or else they incorporate a prism, like binoculars, which allows the light to travel a long way within a relatively small casing.

Magnifications vary from around $15 \times$ (where most binoculars leave off) to $60 \times$ or $70 \times$. Any more than this and you are dealing with an astronomical telescope, in every sense of the word. Many have a choice of magnifications. Some incorporate zoom lenses, others have changeable eyepieces, both systems have their merits and disadvantages. The amount of glass you are looking through with a zoom lens degrades the image definition somewhat and can make it considerably darker. The fixed eyepiece varieties are often first-class optically, though the choice of image size is, of course, limited. Some makes provide a choice of eyepieces ranging from about $15 \times$ through to $60 \times$ and often include a zoom eyepiece as an optional extra. Carrying the full range around with you is heavy work, so the best plan is to settle on the eyepiece you want for the day (a good average is about $30 \times$) and stick with it.

For most uses of a telescope, a tripod is essential. With a heavily built support system you can get away with using higher magnifications in stronger winds, but you pay the price in weight. You can support a scope using a thumb stick and lying back on the ground for stability, but this is only really practical for magnifications of up to $30 \times$, above this the image becomes too unstable. A problem sometimes met, particularly with the prism variety of telescopes, is finding the subject in the first place. The high magnifications mean you have to be very accurate in lining up the scope, or else spend frustrating moments panning to and fro, searching for the right spot. A good way of speeding up the process is to make a simple sight. Set up the telescope to point at an obvious target, such as the top of a telegraph pole. Keeping one eye on the eyepiece, attach a small stick to the front of the scope with tape or Blu-tack, and with both eyes open, manipulate the stick until the tip of it lines up with the top of the telegraph pole as seen with your other eye. To find a subject quickly you need only line up the tip of the stick on it; the view through the 'scope will automatically correspond.

CAMERA KIT

There really is no mystery to camera equipment, despite the dazzling array of models and accessories available on the market. All a stills camera has to do for most types of wildlife photography is show you through the viewfinder precisely what you will get on the film (ie an SLR or single lens reflex camera), and open and close the shutter at the correct speed when you press the button. That is it. Anything more is a refinement. Some of the modern refinements are very useful, others less so; it depends what you want and more importantly, what you need.

My own choice of stills camera has always concentrated on models which, if not completely manual, have allowed me to override all automatic functions. This means that I can have complete control over the photographs I take. It also means that I have only myself to blame if the results are naff, sometimes a hard truth to bear! One of the most important manual features I look for on a stills camera is the film advance. Having owned cameras whose sole method of film advance was a built-in motor wind, I have found to my cost that, with the best will in the world, you never have a spare battery when you need one. It may be more bulky to use a separate motor wind, but it is infinitely more practical to have the choice of both systems when necessary. This is especially true for wildlife photography. Some animals object to the noise of a motor wind, others are more likely to be disturbed by the movement of your thumb as you wind on manually, if your camera is capable of both methods, you won't be caught short in either eventuality.

The other quality I look for in a stills camera is a robust build. Wildlife photography often entails crawling on your belly over mud and rocks, or scrambling over rough terrain in a downpour. Even with a good camera bag, hi-tech lightweight cameras are generally more prone to suffer under these sorts of conditions than a more basic, sturdy model.

Once you have settled on a camera body then you can consider which lens or lenses to buy. The lens is the business end of any camera, and as such deserves very careful thought before you commit yourself. A very ordinary camera fitted with a first class lens will take first class pictures. The most technologically advanced camera in the world fitted with a dodgy lens will take dodgy pictures. It's that simple. So if you are on a limited budget, economize on the body and spend the money on the glass.

The majority of wildlife photography requires a lens of long focal length, at least 300 mm, and often more. The trouble with telephoto lenses is that they need a lot of light to perform well, something which is often in short supply when working in the field. The best of the range can cope with low light levels, but for lenses which have very wide aperture settings you usually have to pay an extra thousand pounds or so. Like binoculars and telescopes, you get what you pay for. Also like binoculars and 'scopes, zoom lenses are something of a compromise. I'm not suggesting that excellent results cannot be gained by using a zoom, far from it. But compared to a fixed focal length lens of an equivalent value, they will always come out the loser by virtue of the increased amount of glass involved.

Other 'essential' lenses for a wildlife photographer are a wide angle, something like a 28 mm for landscapes, and a medium telephoto, perhaps a 150 mm, which is ideal for some hide photography and certain landscape effects. If you are interested in taking stills of bugs, or other tiny beasties, then you are entering the world of macro photography. I find that photographing butterflies or dragonflies demands a macro lens of long focal length (100 mm), allowing me to remain some distance from the subject and still get a decent size in the frame. The advantage of this becomes clear when you try creeping to within a few centimetres of these creatures.

If this were a book about photography, I would go into detail about flash, f. stops, depth of field and so on. But this isn't a book about photography, so I won't.

Before I leave the subject altogether however, a brief word about cine or video-ography. Domestic video cameras have in most cases taken over from 8 mm or super 8 film cameras. Indeed, the low cost of video has contributed to the fact that more people than ever before have access to machinery which can produce a moving image. My own first cine camera was a super 8 mm, a Christmas gift when I was fifteen years old. I immediately set about producing an epic film on the natural history of the suburban woodland near my Bristol home. It included sequences of kestrel, sparrowhawk, kingfisher, water vole and many more. At least that's what I told every one. True, you had to be something of a wildlife detective to spot these animals in the frame, so tiny were they. But I knew they were there.

My own first experiences mirror, I'm sure, those of many people. Even with today's technology, few video cameras are really designed for recording images of distant, small animals. Though frustrating, this is not to say that such cameras are useless for making very good wildlife films. Producing an interesting video has as much to do with choosing a good story as it has to do with getting great pictures, some would say more so. A beautiful shot of a fox is only as good as the reason you are showing it. However lovely the images, they will soon become boring if you have nothing to say about them.

Before you venture out with your video camera, work out what story you are planning to tell, and how realistically you will be able to achieve your goal. It is a good idea to start off featuring the common, more accessible species. Every animal, however familiar, has an element of its lifestyle or behaviour which is new and fascinating to everyone. Careful research will reveal these elements and provide you with the substance for your work.

Having established *what* you are going to film, you have to consider how you're going to achieve it. Details of how to approach each species will be covered later, but an equally important 'how', relates to the techniques of film making. Another HUGE subject so ... just a few words about the basics. Get your camera steady; the only thing moving should be your subject and that means using a tripod. They are bulky and inconvenient to use, but a steady image makes all the difference when you see your results. Try to resist the urge to pan, tilt or zoom the camera at every opportunity. If you want to use any of these camera movements, be certain you know why before starting the move. What is the purpose of the action? What will it reveal to the viewer that couldn't be shown by individual shots? A pan, for example, is one way of showing a wide vista, but it will be a visual anticlimax if it ends on nothing in particular. Both the start and finish should feature something of interest, or perhaps reveal some sort of visual surprise, such as a mountain range springing up from a flat plain.

Zooms are very handy for varying the size of the image, but awful to watch if used too frequently or unnecessarily. Like pans and tilts, a zoom works best if it has a reason—perhaps revealing a well camouflaged animal, or zooming into a part of a landscape where the creature you are about to feature lives.

Most people who use a movie camera want, at some point, to edit their material together into a logical form. Probably the best tutors for editing techniques and requirements are your TV or the cinema. Watching the manner in which professionally made films are pieced together can tell you a great deal about the sort of shots you will have to get to make a complete sequence. Think all the time about trying to get a variety of shots of the same subject, close-up, medium and wide angle. Don't be tempted to concentrate on close-ups alone, exciting though they may be. Remain conscious of the direction things are travelling in, and try to keep it consistent, otherwise you may end up editing together pictures of a fox which appears to be meeting itself. If you are recording an animal on the move, allow it to come into the frame at the start of the shot, follow it for a while, then allow it to move out of the frame at the end. Don't be tempted to cut the camera too quickly after such a move, allow four or five seconds of 'nothing' at the start and end of all action shots if possible. This slack footage will pay dividends in the editing stage.

My own cine camera is capable of running film from 10 to 150 frames per second (fps). Because 16 mm film is generally replayed at 25 fps, this speed range enables me to film subjects which will then appear to be moving slightly faster than normal (time lapse), or much slower, in fact up to six times slower than life. Though a form of slow-mo can be had with video, it is never quite as smooth and clear as the image which can be achieved with film, and this remains one of the reasons it is still widely used in the making of professional natural history productions. For certain jobs I use a Bolex EL camera (great for long time lapse photography), or one of various high speed cameras, which can run film anywhere from between 500 and 10 000 fps.

The lenses I use range from 5.6 mm, very wide angle, to a 600 mm telephoto which magnifies the image by 24 times and performs well in low light levels. The whole lot is supported by a very sturdy and heavy tripod, to help minimize vibration. The total weight of all the kit which I carry in the field can vary between 12–44 kilos, depending on the task ahead.

For stills I usually use a Canon F1 body with a selection of lenses ranging from 28 to 600 mm.

Section 2

The Mammals

When you think of British wild animals, you probably think of badgers, otters, or foxes. This is a little odd because you are far more likely to see a sparrow, a spider or a snail. That we tend to think of the word as relating only to furry creatures which suckle their young with milk probably has something to do with the general popularity of the more cuddly critters. I am certainly asked where otters may be seen much more often than a rare butterfly or amphibian. One of the reasons mammals are so popular may have something to do with our being able to associate more closely with their lifestyles, given that we are also one of them, or maybe it's just because they are cute. Whichever, they remain enormously popular and frustratingly elusive. Comparatively few people have seen a live badger or otter. The sad fact is most folk only get a glimpse of such enigmatic creatures when they spot them dead on the road.

Because this is not an identification guide, I shall not attempt to describe what a species looks like. Nor will I discuss their behaviour in any detail except where it aids spotting or watching them. Many creatures are best seen at certain times of the year and so a calendar of important events will assist with picking the most suitable time for watching. There are also sections on tracks and signs (including voice, an often neglected aid to discovery), observation and photography.

I have omitted certain species which are rarely visible in the field such as the mole, and others which tend to be creatures one spots either through pure luck, or well organized field trips. These include the cetaceans (dolphins and whales) and certain vagrant species, such as the walrus.

The Otter

(Lutra lutra)

One of the best loved yet least often seen of all British mammals, otters encapsulate all that is thrilling in a wild creature. They are shy, rare, playful, powerful and completely at one with their environment. When I saw my first wild otter, the feeling of elation was completely overwhelming. The view was a poor one, a distant blob with a bow wake, surging through the centre of a Scottish loch, but the quality of that first view is not what matters. What matters is that you have broken the spell, that magical, almost supernatural ability some creatures have of staying invisible.

WHERE AND WHEN

Otters, though widespread, are very rare over most of the British Isles. In some parts of south west England, specifically Devon and Somerset, they are making something of a comeback.

These inland populations, and those of Norfolk and Suffolk, however, are very hard to observe. Even though you find all the signs of otter activity, your chances of spotting the animal are slim. The reasons for this are many. One of the most important is the habitat, which tends to be narrow waterways or lake borders. Otters are such wide-ranging animals, covering large distances every twenty-four hours, that the chances of being in the right place at the right time are low. They also tend to be more active during the evening and night.

The habitats most conducive to otter observation are coastal waters and tidal lochs. Here, they tend to be much more active during the day and use large, open stretches of water which are much easier to observe. The only places where you find the combination of good otter numbers living under these conditions are the west coast of Scotland and the nearby isles, the Shetland Isles, and the west of Ireland. The otters found here are precisely the same animal as that found on fresh water, and indeed may well use freshwater rivers and lakes as part of their territory.

Any otter spotted on the sea is often incorrectly called a sea otter. This is in fact a distinct species found only along the coastlines of the North Pacific.

Watching European otters in coastal water can be achieved at any time of the year, depending on the amount of disturbance the animals encounter. I have had greatest success during the autumn, winter and spring. Though I have seen many otters in summer, the views have tended to be briefer and confined to the early or late part of the day. I believe this shift in daily activity is due to an increase, albeit slight, in human activity. It takes very little disturbance to convince these creatures that they would be better off hunting during the night. Otters live and breath with the rhythm of the tide and wind. Anything that moves out of step with that rhythm takes time to be accepted, and time is something we humans seem to have little of.

Because otters have no set breeding season, their courtship and rearing of young has little bearing on when you should venture out to watch them. A far more important element in the search for this animal is the type of coastline. Though otters can turn up anywhere, they much prefer a territory which includes plenty of on-shore opportunities for making a holt, wide stretches of fairly shallow water thick with weed and regular spots where it is easy to enter or exit from the sea. An ideal habitat on the Scottish coast would include forest which came to within 100 metres of the water, plenty of mossy boulders which could provide nooks and crannies for holts, and a shore-line made up of sloping rocks with plenty of weed. The only truly essential element of all these is a rich feeding ground, all the others simply make life easier for the otters. In areas where woodland and boulders are scarce, holts are often formed in peat overhangs or enlarged rabbit burrows. I have even heard of otters using gaps under buildings and culverts under major roads.

TRACK AND SIGN

There are two main ways of telling that an otter has called: runs and spraints. Regularly used otter runs are very distinctive, and no other British animal produces a path quite like them.

When an otter walks or trots, it keeps its tail and body clear of the ground, but only just, and its broad, smooth feet eventually wear a remarkably rounded, flattened track. I always feel that measurements for such features are pretty hard to apply in the field, but as a rough guide, the tracks are rarely any wider than the sole of an adult-sized Wellington boot. Where the tracks push through low shrubs or long grass, they are almost cylindrical, all sides worn smooth by lithe wet bodies. Runs may evolve because they provide an overland short-cut across a headland; in freshwater habitats they may be a means of joining regularly used stretches of water. They may lead to holts, or to sprainting points, or they may simply meander along the bank of a lake or river. A good (and obvious) sign that you have found an otter run is if it leads to water. Watch out for tracks made by waterfowl, which tend to be more ragged, or those made by mink, which are much smaller.

At intervals along some runs you will come across broader areas of flattened ground. This is where the animal has had a good back-scratching, coat-drying roll around. These patches are often created beneath overhanging vegetation, from long grass or reeds to bramble bushes and bracken. Where the runs pass beneath barbed wire fences or over the thorns of blackberry sticks, I have rarely found any dislodged otter hair. This is pretty unusual, because animal hair snagged at suitable points along runs is often a very good guide to its owner; the lack of hair, therefore, may well be indicative of otter activity. Otter hair can be recognized by its dark brown or creamy colour (the hair on the main part of the body is dark, but pale on the belly and chin), and because it is incredibly fine. Otters have no layer of blubber and depend instead, on their fur for insulation and waterproofing. Consequently, their coat has to be very dense to keep out the elements. I have been told that there is as much hair on a 2.5 cm square of otter as there is on a whole cat.

Another distinguishing feature which may be found along otter runs is their spraint. This is the name given to the small amounts of faecal matter which the animal leaves as a smelly message, a calling card for the benefit of other otters who may pass along the same route. It is also the sign which is most helpful to the human observer. From it you can tell how recently and regularly an otter has been using the territory, and sometimes even make a good stab at guessing the age and sex of the creature.

Otter spraint is even more distinctive than an otter run. The colour is very variable, from inky black to pale yellow, depending on the animal's last meal. Those found along fresh water habitats tend to be darker than those found on the coast. At first glance spraints more closely resemble bird droppings than anything produced by a metre long mammal, usually taking the form of an irregular splodge of viscous material. Unlike most bird droppings, however, there are no white bits in the oily mix. A closer inspection may reveal some food remains within the splodge, perhaps some fragments of fish bone or crushed crab shell. But the deciding feature of otter spraint is its smell. Imagine the smell of good, sweet hay, now add a hint of fish and a touch of spice. Voila, zat iz ze spraint. I do not find it in the least bit offensive, in fact it is quite a pleasant scent. Now, it may be that I am a little odd, but having tested the smell on several folk, the general consensus is that it is not nasty, and that cannot be said about many other faeces.

The level of moisture in a spraint gives an indication of its age: the older they are the dryer they get. There are several factors which can affect this; rainfall, temperature, and whether the spraint is protected from these conditions by something like a bridge.

Because there are so many variables it is very hard to provide a truly accurate guide, but as a rule of thumb, a steaming spraint is very fresh, anything with bubbles which are bursting on their own is no more than an hour old; bubbles which burst easily when touched with a small stick indicate an age of between one and three hours; a tough leathery surface is formed after four to six hours; and beyond that you can make a guess based on how dry the spraint is. Very old spraints may be nothing more than a small pile of fish bones or crushed crab shell, with all the oily material washed away. Even these remains will retain something of the tenacious scent described earlier.

Estimating the age of an otter from its calling card is even trickier and not at all an accurate science in the field. The most obvious indicator is size, but unfortunately even the largest dog otter can produce a very feeble spraint. You can sometimes tell when a bitch is being accompanied by a cub or cubs, as the offspring are often compelled to spraint very close to the spot where their mother has done so. Such an event is revealed by the presence of one large plus one or more small deposits in close proximity. I have often observed dog otters scraping the ground with their fore feet at sprainting stations, which are situated on turf or soil, but have never knowingly seen a bitch do the same. Such scrapes may then be indicative of the animal's gender. Male otters do not scrape the ground every time they leave their mark, and this further adds to the chances for confusion. Actual spraint size varies tremendously, an average being about the size of a man's thumbnail, up to the size of the final thumb joint.

Sprainting points are by no means restricted to the edges of well-worn paths. Otters often leave the water to spraint on bankside features, some of which are obvious, others less so. In coastal habitats they tend to use places such as rocky outcrops and promontories, frequently where some short grass or moss has gained a hold. Indeed, the look of the coastal vegetation can often lead you to a sprainting point, because the repeated deposits of fishy leftovers provide a fertilizer which encourages a more lush, green growth, often clearly visible from some distance away. In fresh water habitats the classic site to find an otter spraint is under a bridge. This is one of the few occasions where a 'classic site' really is the best place to start looking, though only under bridges which have a suitable platform for hauling out and leaving a mark. Others may be on bank verges, particularly where overhanging vegetation shields the site from general view, and sometimes on large sloping rocks in the centre of fast moving streams.

Otter footprints are rarely of much help for tracking, because you rarely find them. This has a lot to do with the sort of ground the animals walk across (often rocks or grass), and a little to do with the shape of an otter's foot—broad and flat without well protruding claws. I have seen otter prints on wet mud and sandy beaches, but have never been able to discern clearly the webs between the toes. An adult print is about as wide as the length of a man's thumb, and on a clear one you can discern the pad, plus five distinct toes on the forefoot. As is always the case with animal footprints, good examples are rare, and so the general, indistinct, circular form, and the size and the location in which it is found are the most effective guides.

Otter holts are variable in both appearance and location. Because the animal is not properly equipped for digging, they are never very elaborate excavations, and are often no more than an occupied space between rocks or an enlarged rabbit burrow. The first sign of an active holt is a track (bearing the distinctive features described earlier) leading to a suitably sized hole. This is at least 15 cm across, though often very irregularly shaped. The most active sites usually have a nearby sprainting point, a very smooth area around the entrance hole, and possibly the remains of vegetation collected for bedding. Where possible, otters will pull up grass, moss and other material with their mouths and carry it down into the holt, and this material is occasionally changed for fresh linen. The use of bedding with otters seems to me to be somewhat sporadic and may be linked to seasonal or breeding behaviour.

Unlike many other mammals which use subterranean dens, otters rarely remain faithful to a single holt, but instead move from one to the next fairly randomly. In one territory, which was shared by two adult females, an adult male and various sub adults, I found seven active holts, and many others which had been used at some point in the past six months. Most of these were located amongst large, mossy boulders, one in a peat overhang, and another beneath an old stone wall. The one occasion a holt is used for an extended period is when it contains young cubs. I have never noticed any peculiar feature which distinguished a nursery holt from any other, and have only found such retreats by closely observing the behaviour and movements of adult female otters which I suspected of having cubs.

SENSES

From the field naturalist's point of view, an otter's keenest sense is smell. Whether on land or sea, they manage to keep a nose out for danger most of the time, and depending on wind conditions, can pick up human scent from some considerable distance. Their sense of hearing is pretty good, too, though it seems to be sharper on land than in the water. They are more likely to respond badly to high-pitched sharp sounds than low frequency noises. Eyesight seems to be generally poor, and there have been many occasions when I have been within a few metres of an otter which has only detected my presence once the wind has carried my scent across its path. From my experience a wet otter seems able to see more clearly than a dry one, perhaps the water on the surface of the eye helps with visual acuity. Otters also have a very well developed sense of touch. With long whiskers and sensitive feet they are able to detect prey in water of very low visibility.

SOUND ADVICE

Otters have a wide range of vocalizations, both as cubs and adults, and many of these sounds carry some distance across water or land. One of the most distinctive and persistent is that produced by the cubs when they have lost touch with their mother. Bird-like is the best way of describing the thin, high-pitched, shrill whistle which is emitted at a frequency of roughly one a second. It is best mimicked by whistling through your teeth. Written phonetically, 'Pseep' is the closest approximation I can come up with. If you are familiar with the whistle of an oystercatcher, then the two have a very similar quality, though the otter's voice is not quite as loud or penetrating. The cub's whistle is sometimes very difficult to pin-point, particularly when a strong wind and high sea are rumbling, but with patience it is usually produced frequently enough to give you a fair chance of locating the animal. The female otter also emits a squeak, which is lower pitched and less frequent than that of the young cub, and is a call most likely to be produced when the bitch has lost track of her offspring.

The other call most likely to be heard in the field is a chattering whistle, almost invariably associated with two or more otters coming together or playing or fighting. I have heard it when cubs have been indulging in a bout of rough and tumble, when two or more families of otters have come together, and also when the paths of adult male and female have crossed. It comprises a random trill of whistles and short screeches that vary in pitch and intensity according to the age of the creature and the atmosphere of the encounter.

OBSERVATION

Otter watching can be achieved actively or passively, depending on your preference and the habitat and conditions involved. I have found that in fresh water locations, a passive method is most successful. This usually entails finding a suitable hiding place along a waterway known to be well used by the animals, and waiting. And waiting. And waiting. Night watches are likely to be more productive than those during the day, but this limits your vision considerably. One of the greatest difficulties faced using this technique for observation is finding a water course which allows you a clear view and at the same time ensures your scent is blowing away from any otter approach route.

A passive vigil can also be conducted on the coast, and by choosing a promontory or headland which overlooks a stretch which is known to be regularly used, you stand a very good chance of seeing an otter. But the most successful method of observation in coastal habitats is an active one. By stealthily covering larger areas of an otter's home ground, you stand a much better chance of bumping into the animal.

An otter's keen sense of smell dictates that you must remain constantly aware of the wind direction. If you get into a position where the wind is likely to carry your scent across the water ahead of you, then cut inland until the conditions are more favourable.

Despite relatively poor eyesight, an attentive otter will pick out your outline if you are walking on the skyline. Some hilly habitats allow you to walk freely with very little fear of this happening, but it pays to keep a careful eye on the line between the water's surface and yourself, nonetheless. In flatter habitats, keeping your outline hidden is much more of a problem, and can often only be achieved by moving in a low crouch or retreating well inland.

Like many animals, otters seem to be sensitive to the behaviour of the other creatures which inhabit their watery world. By disturbing a redshank or a heron, you increase the risk of frightening off the animal you set out to see before you even had a clue that it was anywhere nearby. It pays to move stealthily and slowly the whole time. If you do accidentally disturb a bird or other natural sentinel, pause for a while, and allow things to settle before moving on.

As you walk you should be looking in two areas. The first, and most likely, point of contact is the water's surface. Despite their size, otters can remain remarkably inconspicuous on the water. If you are lucky enough to venture out on a near windless day, you have an excellent chance of picking out the dark form and shining ripples produced as the animal makes its way across the surface between dives. Unfortunately, however, near windless days are few and far between on the Scottish coastline, and you are much more likely to have to deal with choppy water. The dark peaks and troughs of waves provide a perfect camouflage for a swimming otter, which allows only a small section of its tail, a bit of bottom, and the top of its head to float. There are two brief moments when the swimming profile shows up a little more: during a dive and when surfacing. Just before diving, an otter will take a deep breath, whilst raising its head and the front part of its body clear of the surface. The last part of the dive often reveals the tail, which flicks up almost vertically before disappearing. When the animal comes back up, its head and shoulders bob up clear of the water before settling back into the low-lying mode. Both actions can be eye-catching and the merest suggestion that something has moved on the water is worth a second look.   Otters spend a lot of time foraging along the edge of the coast, particularly amongst seaweed, which provides an even better camouflage than the waves. When feeding in this sort of situation, the animals usually keep their dives short, with much swirling of the tail and rolling of the body. On calm water such movement can show up well, but in the slightest wind the floating weed becomes a mass of swirling, flapping shapes any one of which may look a bit like an otter. The best clue under these conditions is the animal's serpentine grace which, even in the most turbid seas, is distinguishable from the waving weed.

An animal which suspects danger is like a ghost, allowing its body to sink below the surface, lying motionless amongst the floating weed, and diving with barely a ripple. If you have been discovered by this species before you have spotted it, your chances of a sighting are slim.

The other area which you should constantly check as you make your way along the coast is the shoreline up to the high-tide mark. When an otter catches a meal which is too big to cope with easily whilst floating on the water, it will invariably head to the shore where it can haul its prize out to feed. Here, the colour of its wet fur and low, sleek shape blend so perfectly with the weed and rock that distinguishing its form can be very tricky. Regular pauses to scan with binoculars will pay off, as will close attention to the behaviour of some other coastal inhabitants. When otters feed on shore, they frequently attract the local scavengers who are keen to clear up the leftovers. Hooded crows, herring and black-backed gulls, and even eagles sometimes hang around and are more conspicuous than their mammalian provider. The typical posture adopted by a bird, which is watching an otter feed, is a nervous vigil from a nearby rock, constantly looking down.

Some other animals give clues to an otter's whereabouts. Gulls and sea eagles will sometimes interrupt a direct flight to circle and scrutinize what may be an easy meal of fishy leftovers below. Seals very occasionally hover in the water just off-shore to watch an otter, and some small birds give alarm calls. The latter can be very helpful in locating a sleeping otter, as it lies, curled up on a rock or weed for a snooze. Wrens sometimes hang around the sleeping form and emit a low-intensity ticking alarm, and I have seen meadow pipits rise up in alarm for the same reason. A sleeping otter can be harder to pick out than a feeding one, particularly if still wet, as neither movement nor colour offer a clue at distance. As the fur dries, it becomes fluffy, rather than the sleek 'arrow heads' formed on a wet coat, and turns a lighter shade of reddish-brown. Though it is still a good match for the general background, careful scrutiny will pick out the contrasting texture and hue against the rocks and weed.

Otters offer the field naturalist one great advantage: they dive. Each time the animal is underwater, you can move without fear of being spotted, smelled, or heard. The average hunting dive lasts about 35 seconds, but this period is very variable. It depends on the water depth, the type of quarry, the size and age of the otter, and the success of the dive. If a small fish or crustacean is discovered, the otter will surface and feed on it whilst floating, but a larger meal is always brought onto the shore. When the otter dives, it gives you an opportunity to walk or run in the same direction as it has been moving, but only for about 20 seconds, and always keeping an eye on the water for the animal's return. After 20 seconds, or as soon as you see the otter again, stop, crouch down, and keep quiet. With practise and good fortune, you can predict when and where the otter is about to come ashore and get close to the spot beforehand. The subsequent views of this beautiful animal feeding can be a privilege indeed.

Other pointers that may indicate the presence of an otter are the sound of water splashing, and breathing. It may seem crazy that the sound of an animal sloshing about in a rough sea can be picked out, but it can, and sometimes from some considerable distance away. I can only attribute this to the otter's irregular movements catching the ear against the backdrop of the constant rise and fall of waves. I have located the animals many times using this method, and often in quite big seas with strong wind. The breathing, on the other hand, is only audible under much calmer conditions or at very close proximity, but can be a great help when the otter is hunting in thick floating weed. Often there is a sudden exhalation upon surfacing, sometimes followed by one or two blows which sound as though the animal is clearing its nostrils of water, and ending with a sharp intake just before diving.

If you are doing a lot of otter watching, there will be times, regardless of how careful you are, when the creature smells, hears, or sees you. In this event there is nothing to be done apart from keeping completely still, even for some time after the animal has apparently disappeared. Some time can mean at least five or ten minutes, the reason being that you are almost certainly being watched. Despite having a fear of man, otters are very inquisitive, and many will retreat 100 metres, then hang motionless whilst sniffing the air and watching the shore. When doing this they are often very, very hard to see, but it is essential that you give them time to relax. Once they settle, they often slip away unseen, but at least they leave with nothing to confirm their suspicion of you.

PHOTOGRAPHY

I do not usually use a tripod for stills photography of this species, depending, instead, on convenient rocks as a means of supporting the camera and lens. Otters do not like movement coming from a suspicious looking object, and a motorwind, or automatic film advance helps reduce this. It may pay to 'blimp' the camera, ie, cover it in sound-proofing material, as the sharp sound of the shutter or camera motor can alarm your subject.

Many of the habitats and hours of activity otters keep to, can present a problem with light levels. I have always used a relatively slow slide film (usually 50–64 ASA) for maximum detail in the images, but must confess to many missed opportunities due to low light. Whether you choose to sacrifice picture quality by using a fast film, or photographic opportunities by picking a slow, high quality emulsion, is a very personal decision.

For cine or video photography, a tripod is a must. Use a set which can be kept low and levelled easily, as you will need to conceal your outline and work quickly once the otter is nearby. Never move if you are being watched, or if a feeding otter pauses whilst chewing; like many mammals otters do this to listen out for danger. When you want to move, whilst the otter is underwater, give yourself plenty of time to settle the camera before it surfaces again.

The Badger

(Meles meles)

Badgers share the otter's distinction of being enormously popular, despite the fact that most people have never seen one, or if they have it has been a road casualty. The instantly recognizable features and bearish, bumbling nature have earned them a special place in the hearts of many

At least one good friend of mine included a badger watch in the process of courting his wife. It has to be said that a dark woodland in the chill of night is a wonderful place to get to know someone a little better: there's no struggle to invent witty and intelligent conversation (no talking allowed); there's no embarrassing failure on the dance floor (strictly no movement); there's every reason to sit close to each other (marauding nocturnal lions and vampires) and there's an experience shared after the event. And then, of course, there are the badgers.

WHERE AND WHEN

Badgers are found in most parts of mainland Britain across a wide variety of habitats. Typically, they are creatures of mature woodland with nearby pasture, but I have filmed them in locations as diverse as marshland and city centres. Population strongholds still exist in the south and south west of England, and the strongest urban populations I know of are in the eastern counties.

Badgers survive wherever there is sufficient food and a place to establish a sett. Sadly, some people still delight in torturing these inoffensive beasts with dogs and spades, and badger baiting has been a significant factor in decimating local populations. Road casualties also take a hefty toll each year, but despite all these losses, old brocky somehow manages to hold his own, and in some cases, flourish.

Because they lead a largely nocturnal existence, badgers present something of a challenge to the field naturalist. Their year is predictably structured: mate, overwinter, give birth, mate again, raise young, feed well, mate, etc. The least productive time for badger observation is midwinter. Though they do not hibernate, they do spend a great deal of time below ground through the colder months, particularly if snow cover makes foraging difficult. I once had the good fortune to film a sett in Essex which had been protected and observed by one man for over thirty years. The badgers here were used to popping out for a peanut snack each evening, proffered by their benign human guardian, and would even venture out when snow covered the ground. But despite a guaranteed meal, even these badgers were much less active in winter than at more temperate periods in the year.

The breeding history of these animals is not only fascinating, but significant to the wildlife observer. There are two main periods when mating may take place. The first, and most active, is shortly after the cubs have been born in late February. The second occurs in late autumn, around October, and appears to be less intense. But whichever mating is successful, the female badger puts the development of the fertilized egg on hold until early winter, a process known as delayed implantation. If you are lucky enough to witness a mating taking place, the date of the act plays little or no part in the subsequent birth date of the cubs. They remain underground for the first five or six weeks of life with their mother and make their first bumbling forays into the night air in mid-April. The earliest I have seen cubs above ground is 11 April in a Somerset woodland, and the animals did little more than trip over their own feet for ten minutes before disappearing back underground.

The very best months for badger watching are May and June. It is during this period that the cubs are most active, though still relatively

afraid to leave the security of the immediate vicinity of their underground home for any length of time. Evenings are at their longest which further enhances your badger watching success, because the animals are far more likely to show themselves in good light. During July and August, the cubs spend more time following their mother on foraging trips, though may still hang around the sett immediately after emergence, and, as the autumn progresses, the whole clan grows more and more difficult to observe.

For observation of adult badger activity, early to mid–March can provide some very good results. At this time the adult males are showing a great deal of interest in the females, and it is also the time when many adolescent males and females go for great hikes around the territory, foraging to make up for the winter's lean times. It may be that maturing males are compelled to search for pastures new; despite leading a highly social existence, mature boar badgers, related or otherwise, can be extremely intolerant of each other.

I personally prefer a woodland habitat for badger watching, because it offers certain advantages in the form of natural cover. More open sites can be more tricky to observe if the animals are wary, though setts on downland and in open fields do remain lighter for longer into the evening. Mature forests often harbour large clearings surrounded by trees, and a sett in this sort of habitat is ideal to watch. Hedgerow setts can also provide good views, though finding suitable cover for the observer can be hard.

TRACK AND SIGN

Badgers leave a lot of clues as to their whereabouts. Given that they have very few enemies apart from human beings, they do not have to be pre-occupied with a constant struggle to hide. Clues come in the form of tracks, runs, dung pits, hair, snuff holes and, of course, the setts themselves. Most, if not all, of these are very distinctive, and once familiar are difficult to confuse with the signs of any other European mammal.

Badger tracks show up well in damp soil, and certain features may persist in even the driest of grounds. This is largely due to the animal's long, strong claws which are often used for digging or scraping for food as well as general movement. A perfect badger print reveals five toes, almost in a straight line, and distinctive deep claw marks in front of each. The size of a fore-footprint varies according to age and sex, but an average adult would span the length of a man's thumb in width and from claw tip to back of the pad, about the same. This gives the whole print a very square look. Claw marks alone are a more commonly seen track, but even these are distinctive. No other European mammal leaves such regularly spaced, evenly staggered scratch marks. Often, it looks as though someone has used a five-toothed comb to scrape the earth or tree stump against which the animals have stretched.

These scratch tracks are often found at points along badger runs. Badgers frequently use the same pathway, time and again, between the sett and a favourite foraging area. Often the ground is worn completely bare by the repeated comings and goings, though across fields of pasture they are revealed by a clearly defined path of shorter, worn vegetation. Such paths may be used by generations of animals, and often by many other species, including us. They are usually about the width of two booted feet side by side, or wider. They generally take a direct route between two well used locations. Though worn smooth, they are never as polished looking as an otter's run.

Where runs go up through hedges or steep banks, they are worn bare by the repeated scrapings of clawed feet struggling to get a good hold. These sites are often a good place to search for the parallel marks left by the claws. Paths may even cross short stretches of water, and around my home on the Somerset wetlands, many of the badgers cross the ditches every night to get to and from the sett. Where a badger path meets a road, it invariably continues on the other side, and it is this stubborn indifference to man's hostile world that accounts for many badger deaths. Such crossing points are rarely directly opposite each other, and you may have to walk some way along the roadside to pick up the trail of the animal once more.

There are many factors which help to distinguish a badger path, and these include dung pits. Badgers are unique in the way they deal with their waste matter. The single most diagnostic feature of badger dung is that it is done in toilets. This conjures up images of a queue of brockies, lining up outside a public convenience, but these resourceful animals build their own. Dung pits are found beside well used paths, around the sett, or along any natural feature, such as a hedgerow or woodland edge, which the animals regularly visit. They are especially common where the boundary of two clan territories meet and represent a sort of smelly borderline. Here and elsewhere in the territory they are used by all members of a clan and help to confirm the solidarity of the group. The size of each pit is roughly as wide as a man's hand and roughly a finger's depth. Don't ask how I know!

The dung within varies in colour from earth brown (the most common hue due to the animal's main diet of worms) to black or even purple if they have been feeding on berries. Indeed, a close scrutiny of dung pits reveals a great deal about the badger's diet, and I have stirred up everything from hazelnuts to plum stones in them. The form of the dung is quite indistinct, more closely resembling a pile of wet mud than an animal dropping.

Another common sign, found where a path passes beneath a barbed wire fence, is hair. Usually on the lowest strand, the coarse fur is easy to identify by virtue of its colour, which, perhaps surprisingly, is not grey but creamy white at the base, followed by a black band, and pale again at the tip. Where badgers pass repeatedly against the lowest strands of a wire fence rusting is also likely to occur due to the repeated abrasion from damp bodies.

Badgers have many foraging styles, the most common being a gentle amble in search of earthworms across short grass. Where they detect a worm which retreats underground, they often pursue it, which leads to the creation of snuff holes. These shallow digs are frequently concentrated in food-rich areas, much to the consternation of some lawn-proud gardeners. It is worth remembering, however, that some other species create shallow feeding depressions, including foxes and rabbits. Most badger snuff holes are recognizable by the deep, well spaced claw marks around their periphery, and by their width which is usually greater than the digs created by other species—roughly the same width as a man's hand (about 8 cm).

For prolonged observation of this species, you will need to find a sett. The most likely clue to follow is a well worn path, and I have found many setts by this method alone. Badgers create the most impressive natural earthworks likely to be encountered in the European country-side. Some of the setts I know have at least fifty entrance holes and over the generations, the badgers using them have moved literally tonnes of soil and rock. Smaller setts than this are more common but all have distinguishing features. First is the size of the holes. The largest I have seen would have comfortably taken a small boy, but more usually they are about 40 or 50 cm across. If it looks big enough to stick your head in, it's either a badger or a fox hole. The two can be told apart by the badger's habit of collecting bedding material, remains of which are often in the spoil heaps, or piled up outside the entrance.

Bedding is used in every sett, but remains are more obvious at some than others. A careful search of a likely looking site should, however, always reveal some foreign vegetation strewn nearby. Bedding is changed throughout the year, and the badgers will respond to any glut of suitable material such as hay or dry dead leaves. If ready-cut bedding is not available, they will tear up long grass, dog's mercury, or any other available plant-life that will make a comfy pillow. Areas of greenery which have been plundered in this manner are a further aid to confirming the identity of the sett's occupants.

Quite apart from the bedding and the scale of the earthworks, a badger's smell also helps to make an accurate identification. There is very little that we come in contact with on a day to day basis which is anything like it. The word musky springs to mind, but then this could describe any number of animal scents. Imagine some rather stale human body odour, add a hint of sweet grass and a dash of ammonia. Now you're getting close. This concoction does not smell as bad as it might sound. It plays an important part in badgers' social lives and is liberally distributed around the area surrounding the sett. The main scent gland is situated near the animal's anus, and as well as marking the ground, clan members often mark each other with its pungent contents. I have had the very great privilege of being scent marked both by hand-reared and wild badgers, and can testify that the immediate effect is quite powerful. The scent is not as enduring as that of an otter or fox, and an old, abandoned sett quickly looses any brocky fragrance. Even active setts may lack any strong odour in or around the holes, but a nose-to-the-ground search of the area should eventually yield results.

Badgers display a remarkable degree of fidelity towards a sett, and established individuals will use the same group of holes for many years. Movement does take place, particularly with younger animals, or if undue disturbance occurs. Signs of activity are pretty obvious: fresh digging, footprints or scratch marks, a well trodden entrance to a hole and fresh bedding. Cobwebs quickly take over the entrance of an unused hole, but be careful to check all the holes in a group, as it is perfectly normal for the inhabitants to chop and change their favoured exits and entrances during the course of the year.

SENSES

A badger's most important sense is smell. Their great, snuffly noses are not only ideal for seeking out earthworms and plant tubers, but also for detecting the hopeful badger watcher.

Hearing is good, and a stray rustle or cracking twig will send a nervous badger running for cover. That said, a foraging animal creates quite a bit of noise in the process, and can appear to be half deaf until it stops chewing or snuffling.

Sight is average, and depending on the age and wariness of the animal being watched, could be described as poor. In my experience, a static observer, with reasonable camouflage and background cover, will be overlooked even at very close range. I have had well grown cubs tumble right against my feet during a play fight, with their mother no more than 3 metres away.

Like most wild animals, badgers are sensitive to the 'atmosphere' of their surroundings, and if you disturb other creatures whilst settling in before an evening watch at a sett, you substantially reduce your chances of seeing anything at all.

SOUND ADVICE

Badgers have a truly remarkable vocal range, and few sounds are more thrilling than the first whickers and yips uttered from within the sett as evening falls. Whickering is one of those lovely words that perfectly describes the sound an animal makes. It is a rapid, high-pitched chatter usually produced by animals which are involved in play or another form of vigorous social contact. This sound, along with snuffing, which sounds a bit like a sneeze, and is emitted when a badger is nervous, are the two most commonly heard, but there are many more. Particularly associated with mating is a sound I have always described as chuntering. Male badgers mooch around the area surrounding the sett in March and April, producing a low, grumbling call. If you try clearing your throat four or five times a second, you can produce a similar noise. Adult females also emit a higher-pitched version of this call later in the year when they are being followed by their young cubs, and I have always thought of it as a means of keeping the family together through difficult terrain. Cubs come up with an extraordinary variety of calls when they are playing, from the high-pitched whickering, to a complex combination of growls, whistles and squeaks.

Badgers also produce some distinctive mechanical sounds, which can help locate them in a woodland at night. A badger with a purpose gets from A to B with a trotting gait, and this rhythm is very distinctive when heard through undergrowth or dead leaves. The footsteps come in a regular beat of about two a second. Whilst foraging, the animals can make a huge amount of noise, scuffing up leaves and stuffing their noses into the earth. But possibly the most distinctive mechanical sound is scratching. As badgers leave the sett and at points throughout the night, they have a jolly good scratch. Long claws against coarse hair and skin produce the loudest animal grooming sessions I have ever heard. Four or five scratches a second, sometimes continuing for ten seconds or more, are a sure sign that brock is out and about, and very relaxed. This behaviour can be an extremely social affair, and when several badgers get together it often leads to a mutual grooming session which is usually conducted with the incisor teeth. This is much quieter apart from the odd sneeze when bits get up their noses.

OBSERVATION

Badger watching has become something of a national hobby in its own right, with badger groups popping up all over the country to help conserve the animals. Many of these groups are affiliated to a local conservation trust and as such are a very good place to start indulging your interest in these beautiful creatures. The groups will invariably be led by people who have a good understanding of the animals, and will help both you and the badgers survive the early attempts at watching them. Despite their stubborn nature, badgers can respond very badly to human disturbance, particularly if their experiences of dealing with our species have been harrowing in the past. As a benign observer you must always remember that the animals you wish to see may well regard you as a deadly enemy.

The starting point for all badger watching is at the sett. Having discovered an active location, do not expect to watch it the same night; it is always best to do some careful preparatory work first. Golden rule number one is move gently and quietly. Beneath your feet are nervous wild animals and they will respond poorly to disturbance, even during the day. Walk carefully and quietly, if possible, avoiding the direct vicinity of entrance holes, and try to establish which of the entrances look to be most frequently used. Having discovered this, look for a suitable hiding place within 12 or 15 metres of the sett, which will offer clear views.

Criteria for a 'good' hiding place are not simply camouflage, though this is of course important. The human outline can be picked out by badgers and so keeping your back against a stout tree or dense bush helps guard against discovery. Take account of prevailing wind directions and have contingency locations for every likely wind condition. There is nothing worse than arriving at a site to find that the wind has changed and you do not know where to sit. One answer to this problem is to get up a tree. This more or less guarantees that your scent will pass over the badgers undetected, regardless of its direction, but it does offer a rather removed and distant view of the animals. When picking an observation point, bear comfort in mind. You are likely to be sitting motionless in this spot for at least three hours. This can give rise to a peculiar disorder known as 'numbum' if you don't pick your seat carefully.

Badgers are quite partial to a snack just after they leave the sett and many naturalists exploit this to extend their viewing time. If you are considering using a bit of food bribery to encourage the animals you are watching to hang around, then start feeding them well before your first observations. Badgers will eat all sorts of goodies. Being omnivores, their tastes range from worms and hedgehogs to honey sandwiches. I think that the best food, from the point of view of nutritional value, size, and availability, is peanuts. The variety you can buy to feed the birds is ideal. A scattering of nuts around the sett will keep the inhabitants snuffling about for some time before they go off to forage. This, however, assumes that the badgers know that a peanut, smelling slightly of human hand, is an edible item, so it pays to toss a handful of nuts across the sett each evening, well before you intend watching.

In my experience, feeding badgers low volumes of healthy food has no negative side effects whatsoever. The idea that they will become somehow less wild or even dependent on man does not apply in any but the most extreme cases. The group of thirty or more I worked with in Essex would leave the sett, after a few feeding and grooming sessions, to wander into the suburbs which surrounded their island of woodland. Here they would visit one home in particular, where, quite independently of their human guardian at the sett, two more people laid on the most extraordinary spread. The badgers wandered up to the front door and even into the living room to fill up on all manner of goodies. Given that their natural foraging sites had been virtually all destroyed by housing developments, this bounty represented a means of survival for many of the clan.

The situation in Essex is a rare one. Despite many badgers around the country gracing suburban and rural homes with their presence each night to gobble up a free meal offered by interested humans, most of these animals go off to forage for a natural diet during the rest of the night. A few handfuls of peanuts are nothing more than a very light snack, and the degree of conditioning caused by offering them is negligible. Having said all that, I rarely feed the badgers at a sett the first time I want to watch them. I find that I get a much better idea of who and how many live at the site by conducting a 'zero influence' watch for at least the first few occasions.

Having settled on your observation point, it now pays to prepare a way into the spot. Many woodland setts are surrounded by dead leaves and twigs, and on the night of the watch you are going to want to arrive as quietly and quickly as possible. You should avoid walking on the badgers' tracks because the scent of your footsteps may influence the animals' behaviour. Prepare your own track by clearing the worst of the noisy brash on a path leading at least 9 or 12 metres into the site, making sure you do this for each of the likely watching positions. All of these preparations should be carried out during the middle of the day and never at dusk when the badgers are contemplating coming out.

Leave the prepared site for at least one full day and night, (sometimes the most difficult part for the enthusiastic naturalist). On the night before you intend to watch, keep an eye on the weather forecast. The ideal conditions are a light to moderate wind (in the right direction), fairly warm, and no rain. Quite apart from being the most comfortable conditions for watching badgers, these also offer you the best chance of extended views. In rain, particularly drizzle, badgers will be keen to go off and search for earthworms, and may well disappear without stopping to groom or play. In strong wind, they are much more nervous than at other times, probably because they are less able to hear the subtle cracks and rustles that could warn them of approaching danger. In very light wind conditions, the direction of the breeze can be variable, and having committed yourself to sitting in a prepared site, you may find that the shifting breeze carries your scent across the sett half way through the session.

On the day of the watch, leave plenty of time to get ready and in position. You should be settled at least one hour before the likely first emergence of any badger. The actual time varies greatly according to the individual badgers and the time of year, but play safe, and in summer try to be settled at least two hours before sunset. Other preparations you should make are dressing for the occasion. The most important element for badger watching is silence and so it is imperative that you do not wear 'noisy' clothing. Nylon waterproofs are out, as are many of the synthetic jackets and trousers designed for outdoor wear. The slightest wriggle or shift in this clothing sets up the most atrocious racket. Woollen jumpers, duffle coats, or Loden jackets are all ideal. Wax jackets are fine, but you have to be careful not to let your arms rub against your sides as this does create noise. Ventile, a special weave of cotton, is both waterproof and fairly quiet and a pretty good all-round fabric for the field naturalist's clothing.

Having sorted out what you are going to wear (and dress up warm, you will be very still for a long time), you are almost ready to go. The only added comforts may be an old cushion, some insect repellent on your exposed parts, and a visit to the loo. It pays not to drink a great deal prior to going out on a badger watch.

As you approach the sett, move quietly and pay constant attention to wind direction. At no point should you allow your scent to pass over the area, as a badger may well be awake and sense your arrival even this early in the evening. If you are with someone else, do not talk. As you get to within 12 or 15 metres of the sett, start to move as quietly and stealthily as you would if approaching a visible creature. On reaching your prepared observation site, settle quickly into a position you think you can hold, without shifting a muscle, for at least four hours. And now all you have to do is wait.

Badgers are very sensitive to movement above ground just before they emerge, and even a passing roe deer may frighten them for a while. If you have been throwing peanuts across the sett, the first sign you may have of an animal about to venture forth is the sound of eating. Often, one or two nuts roll down the entrance holes and are eaten as the badger starts to leave. More usually you will hear a gentle snuffling sound as the badger scents the air, or perhaps the odd whicker or yelp coming from just inside an entrance.

It is perfectly normal for badgers to be cautious as they first leave the sett, scenting the air and poking their heads above ground several times before coming out. Cubs are generally less nervous than adults. If you keep getting glimpses of a badger nose, but after half to three-quarters of an hour no animal has emerged, there may well be something wrong, and it is prudent to leave quietly and return another day.

Though badgers can be active well before dark, particularly in the summer months, they are truly nocturnal animals and only really settle down after dark. This makes observation difficult, and though you can use the night observation methods as described in Section 1 of this book, you can also use artificial light for a clearer view. Most badgers will tolerate a dim torch-beam so long as it is introduced to them slowly and carefully. Some people use a red filter across a torch to help dim it, but I have found that virtually any light colour, so long as it is not too bright, will be accepted. Before switching any torch on, allow the badgers to emerge and settle. The torch you are using must have a silent switching system—one which operates by rotating the head is ideal. Turn the light on, covering the beam with your hand, and direct it roughly 3 metres behind the badger you wish to observe. Now slowly expose the beam by drawing your hand away from the front of the torch. If the badger remains relaxed slowly pan the light on to it, from rear to head. If at any point the animal looks alarmed, stop whatever you are doing, but if you do not make any sudden moves to switch off the light or cover it with your hand, often the animal will settle again very quickly. If it is obvious that the badger simply does not like the whole idea, gently cover the beam with your hand and switch off the light, abandoning the torch until another night.

Badgers can be habituated to a human presence, but this takes a lot of time—from weeks to years. Some would argue that it is not in the animals' best interests to consider a human being as benign, but in my experience, a wild badger which gets used to the individual remains very wary of strangers.

Once a badger is comfortable with your scent and presence, it opens up completely new methods of observation, the most important of which is following the animals on foot. Usually when the clan goes off to forage it is a signal that it is time for you to get up gently and leave the sett, but a habituated group or individual will allow you to follow their activity at a reasonable distance. It helps if you always wear the same clothes when badger watching, move in the same way and at the same times, and avoid over-reacting if you are discovered. However carefully you prepare for a watch, there will be times when the badgers smell, hear, or see you. In the short term this discovery is undesirable, but if you intend to watch a single sett regularly (at least once a week, if not more), these exposures are a positive move in the direction of being accepted. I often leave an old bit of clothing, which I have worn during the day, in the woodland adjacent to a sett. The badgers undoubtedly come across it during their wanderings, and it helps to familiarize them to my scent. In fact, many of the old shirts and trousers I have used for this purpose end up as bedding material for an enterprising animal.

At the end of a badger watch, it is important that you leave as quietly and carefully as you arrived, so ensuring a continued trust in you and your actions.

PHOTOGRAPHY

I have very little experience of taking stills photographs of wild badgers, having almost always used cine film. The two disciplines are quite different because cine requires constant light and stills can be achieved using flash photography.

I have met many people who have devised ways of taking stills of badgers at night and they have all independently come up with similar systems. The most common problem they all face is focusing accurately on the subject and framing correctly before pressing the button and firing the shutter and the flash. Most have devised a rig which involves a low-power torch, strapped to a camera gun-mount, which in turn supports the camera and flash system. The torch can be used for framing and focusing and to allow the shutter to be released at the perfect moment. This sort of system can achieve some remarkable results, but it always suffers from a rather flat image as a consequence of the flash being mounted so close to the camera. More elaborate flash systems

Opposite: The docile gaze and full belly of this fallow buck in summer belie the extraordinary transformation which occurs during the rut. It is then that the antlers harden, the velvety skin from them is shed and the male deer adopt the strength and aggressive nature that will be needed to secure a mate.

Above: Badgers may be watched at any time of the year, though spring and summer are the seasons which usually offer the clearest and most extended views.

Left: To photograph a bird in flight, such as this common buzzard, it is sometimes possible to pre-set the focus of the lens on a point just ahead of the action and wait until the animal moves into it. Use of a motorwind can be very handy in this situation.

which provide a side or back light depend on the subject passing through a pre-determined spot. Badgers are quite obliging for this style of photography, because they use traditional setts and paths and their movements can be quite accurately predicted. Methods such as infra-red beam breakers, trip wires, and pressure pads have all been used to fire cameras remotely as a badger moves through the desired point. These 'sleeping rigs' are fantastic if you have no fear that your gear may be stolen, and they sometimes provide unexpected results (an infra-red trip switch can't tell the difference between a badger and a roe deer which walks through it).

Cine or video images need a certain amount of constant light. Some modern cameras can operate in very low light, or by using otherwise invisible infra-red light. All these methods can be used at night, but they never reproduce an image with the full range of colours obtainable with full spectrum light. The only way to achieve this is to habituate the badgers to a constant artificial light source or sources. This has to be done with time and care, but can eventually provide some wonderful images.

The ideal situation for filming is a sett which is within 100 metres or so of a power source, otherwise you have the added hassle of keeping a generator running the whole time. Try to attach the lamps you are using to trees and keep them and their wiring as inconspicuous as possible. This not only prevents theft but more importantly prevents inquisitive people from following your equipment and unwittingly disturbing the badgers. Lights should be operated on dimmer switches and very gradually increased over a period of weeks. It is important that you continue observations as this introduction takes place and that you have some way of controlling the lights from your watching position. My own lighting rigs normally comprise four lamps, with a total output of 4000 watts at

Left: Though among the more elusive of British mammals, with a careful approach, otters may be watched for prolonged periods. In time they may come to accept the presence of a patient observer and even investigate you.

any one time. Each lamp is mounted on a remote control pan and tilt-head, which allows me to move the beam of the light silently on to activity over a very wide arena. At the slightest hint that the badgers are unsettled I can dim, pan, or switch off the lights from my filming position.

The whole time you are equipping yourself to photograph or film badgers, sound level must be a constant consideration. Use fabric insulation to muffle camera noise and make sure all switches operate silently.

Finally, and most importantly, badgers are very idiosyncratic and the behaviour displayed by one may well be quite different from that of another. If your actions look like causing stress, abandon them at once, and start the search for another group of animals that may be more accommodating.

The Wild Cat

(Felis silvestris)

Many of the wild cat populations in the UK have interbred with feral domestic cats, making it very hard to be sure when you have spotted the genuine article.

Unfortunately, I have never had the good fortune to concentrate on this species in the field and the majority of sightings have had more to do with luck than judgement.

WHERE AND WHEN

Wild cats are restricted to the north, west and central Scotland. Their numbers reached an all time low in this country just before the First World War, when persecution drove them into remote pockets of moorland and hill country. Since that time, more enlightened attitudes have helped this predator expand its range, and this has also been helped by the increased planting of conifer woodland. The young plantations offer an ideal hunting habitat, often harbouring good populations of small mammal prey.

It is unusual to spot more than one cat at a time; they are fiercely territorial animals, guarding a hunting area against the possible depletions from other hunting cats. The toms seek out the company of the cats in early spring, but play no part in the raising of the young. Kittens are normally born in May or June and remain with their mother for about five months. A typical breeding den is situated amongst large boulders or in a hollow log. Since cats are ill equipped for digging, they rarely do more than the most superficial of home improvements.

Most of the sightings I have had in daylight have been in the winter months, when the cats are probably forced to hunt for longer periods due to a general shortage of voles and other small mammals. For the rest of the year they are crepuscular or entirely nocturnal, further adding to the problem of observation.

TRACK AND SIGN

The footprint is very like that of a domestic cat, only a little larger and rounder than most. Those that I have seen, have all displayed four toes with no claw marks.

Dung is typically cat-like, both in look and scent, that is very pungent when fresh. I have found dung varying in colour from dark grey to pale brown, often containing a large amount of mammal hair. The faeces are only rarely buried, and many are left in prominent places such as rocks and logs, much in the same manner as a fox. I have seen a feral cat (a large black-and-white tom) do much the same thing, so confusion is quite possible.

I have never found any cat hair, or knowingly found a well used track, though have had reports of a female wild cat which repeatedly used the same point of entry and exit to a forestry plantation over a period of weeks. The only prey which I have found and could attribute to a wild cat was the inverted skin of a rabbit, largely cleaned of muscle tissue and with small bones chewed.

SENSES

Like their domestic cousins, this species has excellent hearing and sight. A long history of persecution by gamekeepers has forced them to put these exceptional abilities to good use, avoiding any contact with the human race. Their eyesight is particularly well tuned to movement and their sense of smell acute over a great distance; one cat I saw picked up my scent from at least 300 metres away.

SOUND ADVICE

I have never heard a peep out of any of the cats I have seen in the wild, but have heard reports of screams and hisses produced by courting animals. I once heard a captive mother and young producing a purring sound but have never had a report of any sound resembling a 'meow' coming from this species.

OBSERVATION

This is a very tricky animal to watch in the wild. Staking out a known hunting area may pay off, particularly in locations where human disturbance is minimal. Use of an elevated viewing platform, either an existing tree or scaffolding should help avoid detection. Otherwise, similar techniques to those used with foxes should yield results.

The Pine Marten

(Martes martes)

One of the most shadowy and elusive of all the large animals in Europe, the pine marten's restricted range, habitat and behaviour make it one of the most challenging to watch in the wild. My own contact with this lovely member of the weasel family has been limited to the west coast of Scotland, one of their last strongholds.

WHERE AND WHEN

Pine martens are restricted to the wilder parts of Scotland, particularly the north and west, with isolated populations in northern England and north Wales and the west of Ireland. The sort of habitat I would expect to see a marten in is ancient deciduous or mixed woodland, with ample dead trees, boulders, and other suitable retreats for the animal to rest in during the day. Areas of clear, felled coniferous forest are also potentially good country, particularly in years when the vole population is high. The other most likely spot for sighting a marten is around rural human habitations, as these animals seem to like the warm, dry outbuildings, and indeed the food scraps which we may proffer, intentionally or otherwise.

I have seen well grown youngsters in August and newborn kittens in early April. Like the badger, pine martens have delayed implantation after mating most of which takes place in July and August. The young are slow to develop and may take two months or more before emerging from the nest to any great degree.

The best views I have had of adults hunting have all been in mid-summer, in clearings amongst ancient coastal oak forest, and also on areas of clear fell plantations. All have been at dusk and dawn, apart from the odd occasion when I have disturbed a sleeping marten during the day. The nocturnal habits of these creatures are sometimes adjusted when they find a ready food supply, and in remote areas they may become accustomed to visiting a feeding station created by man. Once their trust has been won, they can be extraordinarily tractable, arriving at the same time each day for their meal, and even taking food directly from the hand.

TRACK AND SIGN

The most obvious and prolific signs that martens are in an area are their droppings. Footprints, hair, prey remains, etc, are all very hard to come by in the field and have never really helped me to establish the whereabouts of the animals. I have never found well-worn tracks or runs which I could attribute to this species, almost certainly as a consequence of their random hunting style.

The droppings are fairly distinctive, though could be confused with those from a number of other species, specifically foxes. The greatest differences occur in the shape and colouring of the waste, and also in the scent, which is quite neutral on any but the most fresh, which may be a little musky. The shape and colour differs greatly according to the food taken, which may vary from voles or squirrels to berries and beetles. Any droppings which contain hair are classically 'squiggly', and often dark or blackish. Droppings I have found containing blackberry seeds only remain in one piece until the next rain, when they rapidly start to fall apart. They are all characteristically smaller and less regularly shaped than a fox dropping, and lack the 'foxy' smell.

Pine martens leave their dung in prominent places, such as logs and rocks, and often re-visit these sites to leave a deposit, resulting in quite large collections of dung. I have found marten dung on top of both otter and fox deposits, a sort of battle of the scents you might say.

I have only ever found marten prints on two occasions, both in wet sand adjacent to coastal oak forest. They were long, some displaying five toes, others only four, and all lacked claw marks (I believe that the claws do show under certain damp ground conditions). They were all quite indistinct, probably as a result of the extremely furry pads on the soles of the marten's feet, and were about the same size as a cat's. The most noticeable distinction was the distance between the pad of the foot and the toes, which was greater than any other comparable species' print.

SENSES

Hearing and sight are both very keen. I have never been able to establish how well developed a marten's sense of smell is, though have always approached them downwind as a matter of caution. They seem to use their ears a great deal when vole hunting, striking poses reminiscent of a hunting cat or fox.

SOUND ADVICE

I have never knowingly heard a marten in the wild. However, I was once lucky enough to be treated to an intimate encounter with a couple of captive animals, which, apart from having needle-sharp claws put to great effect when climbing on to my head, also produced low intensity calls from time to time which resembled a form of cat purring.

OBSERVATION AND PHOTOGRAPHY

The martens' nocturnal habits call for dusk and dawn vigils or else a clear full moon. Hunting behaviour can be quite regular and favoured sites are visited time and again where prey is abundant, often at the same time each day. A friend of mine in west Scotland once took me to a site where he had been watching a marten hunting in clear felled forestry land for several evenings in a row. Sure enough, about half an hour after sunset, it arrived on the scene, snuffling and leaping around the many stumps and logs which littered the area. It often stood up on its hind legs to survey the ground, and despite coming to within 18 metres or so, never picked out our hunched forms amongst the bracken.

The Weasel

(Mustela nivalis)

These little carnivores are very close to my heart because I have had the good fortune of living with a hand-reared individual for seven years which allowed me a rare and invaluable insight to the habits of this normally elusive little hunter. Observations of this species in the field are very tricky because of the animal's size, speed and habits.

WHERE AND WHEN

Weasels occur all over England, Wales, and Scotland. I have seen them in habitats ranging from open moorland to thick woodland and at all times of year. Despite hunting regularly by day, weasels are so small that they spend most of their lives hidden from our view, either curled up in a nest, or scuttling along a mouse or vole run, completely concealed by long grass or other natural cover. Most views which I and most other naturalists get of wild weasels are when the little creatures come to a road or track and pop across it. The habitat most conducive to weasel watching is open pasture, because this affords the lowest degree of available cover for the little predator. Even so, views will almost certainly be restricted to unpredictable glimpses.

As they prey on small mammals, though rarely on rabbits, unlike their larger cousin the stoat, they are most prolific where vole or mice populations are high. Indeed, breeding success may relate directly to the abundance of prey species in any given year. Mating may occur in any month from March until July, the young born in the seclusion of a nursery den some two months or so later. Almost all the young weasels I have seen have come from early summer litters, though in years when food is freely available, females may rear two lots of young.

TRACK AND SIGN

Such a tiny creature doesn't leave too many clues. The five-toed footprints are so infrequently found that they offer little in the way of guidance for the field naturalist, and hair is very unlikely ever to be caught on a barbed wire fence or other snag. I have found weasel droppings in the wild, either just outside den sites or occasionally along well used routes, often hidden from immediate view by vegetation or other cover. Each dropping is classically mustelid in shape—elongated and squiggly, invariably dark or blackish, and containing a large percentage of small mammal hair. Well-used dung sites may accumulate a large number of scats or droppings, which have a musty, fairly bitter odour. The only other smell likely to be encountered is produced by this species in times of high alarm. When attacked by a predator (and this includes motor cars), weasels deposit a tiny amount of incredibly potent fluid. Niva, the tame weasel who lived with me for seven years, once sent this smelly message when the family cat got rather too close for comfort. It seemed to take only a matter of a second or two before the whole house was full of the most appalling stench which I can best liken to that made by commercially available stink bombs.

Other signs which may be left by a weasel include prey remains or caches. Despite a huge appetite, weasels may be compelled to store food simply because they haven't the capacity to consume it all in one go. Such hoards are often well hidden within or very close to dens, sometimes in hollow logs, or amongst stony piles and walls. I once found a blackbird nest which had been raided by a weasel, the tell-tale sign being a broken egg shell which bore the puncture points of two tiny but very sharp canine teeth. The distance between the holes was no greater than a centimetre, too small for a stoat or mink, the only other likely culprits.

SENSES

Due to their stubborn indifference to people, a weasel's senses do not greatly affect the field naturalist. My tame weasel had very good eyesight and hearing. He seemed to use his nose when investigating close objects but did not often appear to smell the air. He occasionally left scent marks both with anal glands and by rubbing his chest along slender objects such as branches or armrests of chairs, none of which were detectable to the human nose, which suggests a well developed sense of smell at close range at least.

SOUND ADVICE

Having lived with this species, I have been exposed to their full range of vocal sounds, much of which are very low intensity and unlikely ever to be heard in the field. When excited and in a positive mood, they produce a lovely soft warbling sound, very low in volume and emitted with the mouth closed. When anxious or

aggressive, they make a short hissing, like a burst of air escaping from a beach ball. If you hear this call do not attempt to handle the weasel making it, or you will almost certainly receive a very painful bite. A stressed weasel makes a shrill, scratchy squeak, something like the sound produced by a brown rat.

Mechanical sounds of the animal moving through vegetation are rarely an aid to spotting this species in any but the closest of encounters.

Small birds, especially wrens, tits and chaffinches may mob a hunting weasel, though never in a very intense manner. By watching the gaze of birds which appear to be anxious, it may be possible to pin-point this little hunter.

OBSERVATION AND PHOTOGRAPHY

My filming of weasels has always involved captive animals, all of which have been hand-reared as a consequence of losing their natural mother. Weasels raised in this manner become quite tractable, though are always potentially aggressive. Diminutive they may be, but a bite from one is very painful, especially as they have a knack of getting to the parts other creatures cannot reach. Live trapping of adult weasels causes a high degree of stress to the animal and should be avoided. They are a highly strung species and will die of starvation if left hungry for longer than twenty-four hours.

The Stoat

(Mustela erminea)

Stoats are found right across the British Isles and Ireland in an even greater variety of habitats than their smaller cousins, the weasels. They are also a little easier to watch because of their larger size and habit of hunting in more open areas.

WHERE AND WHEN

Mountain top to lowland pasture—indeed, anywhere there is sufficient food—will provide a stoat with a home. Because of their size (about twice that of a weasel), they are able to tackle larger prey, such as rabbits and adult rats, though will hunt smaller creatures regularly. They are unable to follow voles and mice down their burrows as the weasel does, so they are more likely to be seen hunting in full view where the vegetation is sparse. In areas where hunting is good, such as a rabbit warren or vole rich pasture, they may return time and time again to the same place, often at the same point in the day. I have seen stoats catching voles, rats and rabbits.

Stoats have delayed implantation so that despite mating in the spring and early summer, the young are not born until the following spring, usually around April or May.

TRACK AND SIGN

These are very similar to those of the weasel, but with slightly larger droppings, footprints and sometimes larger species in prey remains. Stoats quite often kill birds, the remains of which may be identified by the way in which the feathers have been removed. The end of each quill, particularly primary and secondary feathers from the wing, have a frayed, chewed look to them, and are not usually as widely scattered as those found at a fox kill.

SENSES

Eyesight and hearing are good. Though inquisitive, stoats tend to be wary of humans, responding negatively to sudden movement and obvious outline.

SOUND ADVICE

Despite many sightings in the wild, I have certainly never heard this species calling in the wild. I once filmed a captive stoat, which occasionally produced a short hissing sound. I took this to be a warning that I was getting too close.

OBSERVATION AND PHOTOGRAPHY

If you happen to come across a hunting stoat, and you have a better chance of this than of a weasel, it may well be worth revisiting the site the next day. One stoat that took to hunting around our house showed up at roughly the same time each day for about two weeks, often revealed to me by the chattering alarm call of the local wrens. He proved quite indifferent to my presence, and came up to my feet on several occasions.

The Mink

(Mustela vison)

Mink are now very much a part of British fauna. In the areas I have watched them, if left undisturbed, they seem to reach a self-levelling population density, regulated by territorial breeding males and females.

WHERE AND WHEN

This species was introduced to the British Isles via fur farms in the 1930s. It has now spread to almost all parts of UK and southern Ireland. It is enormously adaptable, and because it swims well, can utilize river and sea habitats as well as dryer sites. Almost all of the mink I have seen have been close to some form of water. In coastal habitats they are generally easier to watch by virtue of the lack of available cover. All seem unperturbed by a human presence, except in areas where they have been persecuted.

Some Scottish coastlines provide very good views of mink, as do parts of the Somerset Levels, Devon and rivers throughout southern England. Like many of their cousins, mink are opportunistic hunters, though their habit of following waterways means it is sometimes possible to stake out a suitable area. Favoured sites usually include good vegetation cover on the banks and plenty of areas for denning. These include rock piles, logs, drainage culverts and even piles of bricks or other building material. Most of the dens which I have found have been on the bank of a river or lake, or within 12 or 15 metres of water. Mink will occasionally live away from watery habitats, especially where food is plentiful, such as large rabbit warrens.

Mating usually occurs in early spring, but the young are rarely very active outside the den until midsummer. I have seen young mink, which were still returning to the nursery den after short excursions, in July and August.

Most mink are nocturnal, though they do frequently forage in daylight, particularly in the summer. Most of the sightings I have made have been in early morning or late afternoon and evening.

TRACK AND SIGN

This is one of the few mammals living in Britain and Ireland which regularly leaves good, clear footprints. This can be explained by the mink's habit of skulking along the fringes of water courses where the mud is damp and soft. Indeed, we often see mink following the riverbank which runs alongside our Somerset house, swimming briskly from one bank to the other, and regularly hauling out to forage for frogs or voles. The prints are much smaller than an otter's, with well splayed five toes (although these do not always all show up very well). In fact, it is this splayed look which is characteristic, giving the print an almost flower-like quality. The claws are sometimes distinct from the rest of the toe, but more usually they blend into a single, tear-drop shaped mark.

Their scats are often left in much the same sorts of places as otter sprant, under bridges, on prominent rocks, etc, though one good sniff will soon distinguish them. Unlike the sweet hay smell of otter dung, mink faeces have an acrid scent, which is really quite unpleasant. The look of a mink scat is not unlike otter sprant, though usually more cylindrical and solid. Colour varies a great deal, depending on the last meal, from green to black, and many of the scats contain fish bones.

Mink sometimes create worn runs along the bankside vegetation, but these are never as clear or smooth as those made by otters, neither are they as regularly used. I have found one or two regularly used scat points which were betrayed by the narrow track leading up to them.

SOUND ADVICE

Mink can see and hear well, and they use these

senses all the time for hunting and checking for danger. They sometimes give the impression of being utterly incapable of sensing a thing; I once had one come into one of my portable hides whilst I was filming nesting kingfishers, and walk straight across my feet. This behaviour has far more to do with the animal's inquisitive, stubborn nature than defective sight or hearing. Judging by the way they have approached my inanimate form to get a closer look, they are capable of discerning a foreign object in their home ground, and certainly see movement clearly. Though scent is used during certain hunting styles, it does not seem to be used to locate a threat.

SOUND ADVICE

I have only once heard mink in the wild. It turned out to be an encounter between two males (judging by their size), and was obviously aggressive. The sound which drew my attention to the fracas was a shrill, screeching call, a little bit like the sound you can produce by saying 'pschh' through your teeth, using lots of air and no voice.

OBSERVATION AND PHOTOGRAPHY

Wild mink are very unpredictable in their movements around their territory. Despite keeping quite faithfully to a stretch of water, they are prone to concentrate in different parts of that ground quite randomly, depending on the availability of food. I once filmed, by pure chance, a mink bringing an eel on to the bank of a flooded peat cutting and feeding on it. I returned to the site the next day and was rewarded with precisely the same scenario. The following day, full of cocky confidence I went back to top up on the footage I had gained so far and saw absolutely nothing. The next day was the same. And the next.

It is worth a quick comparison of otters and mink for identification, simply because they are easy to confuse in the field. The massive size difference is not always obvious in choppy water and poor light. A mink, however, tends to swim much higher in the water than an otter, revealing all or most of its body. Mink are also relatively poor divers; they do submerge frequently, but they cannot remain under for the same duration as an otter, an average dive lasting no more than ten or fifteen seconds compared with thirty or so.

The best views I have had of mink have tended to be at the nursery den. This is one area where they can be quite jumpy, and so standard precautions of camouflage or hides and silent watching apply.

Dens are betrayed by trampled areas with mink scats nearby and cosy-looking retreats. The one time I searched for and found a den, I simply walked a water course which harboured a good mink population, searching in hollow trees, gaps between rocks, holes in the bank, indeed anywhere which looked like a suitable hideaway. I finally came across a den, which was betrayed by a vague track leading to it and several black scats littered around the outside. It turned out to contain four well-grown youngsters, which thereafter provided fantastic views as they emerged at various points in the day to have games of tag and rough and tumble on the bank and in the shallows of the pool nearby.

The Fox

(Vulpes vulpes)

Most people have had some experience of a wild fox. They are probably one of the greatest survivors on the planet, covering a vast range from North America to Japan, with feral populations as far afield as Australia. They are one of the natural world's most adaptable carnivores, living in habitats which range from remote mountain and moorland to inner cities.

Their presence provokes a wide range of reactions in people from adoration to hatred or even fear. But whatever you think of them, you cannot deny that they are one of Europe's most dynamic and admirable wild creatures.

Over the years, I have hand-reared and released several orphaned fox cubs, and at the age of ten, I acted in a film called simply *The Fox*, where I played the part of a lad living on Dartmoor during the Victorian period, who finds and befriends a fox which has been caught in a gin trap. To become properly acquainted with the animals that were to appear in the film with me, I hand-reared two orphans that had been brought to a local wildlife park. These early experiences forged a bond and respect for this most charismatic of creatures which remains with me to this day. In short, foxes are fab.

WHERE AND WHEN

The only thing preventing a fox from colonizing an area is lack of food, and their catholic tastes ensure that this precludes very few. Where they suffer heavy persecution from man, they are much more difficult to observe, some of the wildest of wild foxes being in the Scottish hill country where sheep farming has traditionally dictated a high level of control. Perhaps the easiest habitat to watch them in is an urban area, where they often become so used to people that they ignore our presence all together.

Foxes were very common in the area of Bristol where I lived as a child. Each night we would put out a few household scraps and were rewarded by a visit from our friendly vixen, who was often joined by her cubs. These foxes became so used to me that they would take food which lay at my feet and happily tolerate bright lights shining on them from my bedroom window, and the sound of the TV ringing out from the lounge. This ability to adapt to new opportunities is the fox's greatest survival asset.

Foxes that live in the country are more likely to be afraid of man, given the long history of confrontation that has developed as a result of our shared interest in hens and lambs. Foxes can sometimes be a problem with certain types of livestock, but the reputation they have earned as bloodthirsty, maniacal killers is often exaggerated. Yes, they will kill a lot of hens if they get into a hen-house, and if left completely undisturbed, they will, in all likelihood, return and collect every kill. Their response to an easy glut of food is simply governed by the artificial abundance of prey. What they can't eat, they will bury for later use.

Rural foxes occupy virtually every habitat, and their earths can be found in woodland, hedgerow, open fields, mountains and moorland. I have found fox earths in hay barns, sand-dunes, under buildings and virtually any other suitable dry site.

The fox's year runs a predictable course in Britain. During December and January they court and mate. Cubs are born in March but remain underground until late April, early May. This is when the fox family is at its most obvious, with the cubs coming out to play throughout the day, and the parents working overtime to keep their offspring well fed. In June the cubs slowly become more crepuscular and nocturnal, and though still active by day, are generally more nervous. It is now that the youngsters start to follow their mother on hunting trips, so that by July and August the young fox's behaviour closely resembles that of their night-wandering parents. As the autumn approaches, many fox families start to split up, the vixen and dog harrying and chasing their well-grown cubs out of the territory as the need to mate rises within them once again.

The best time for fox watching is mid to late May. The activity of both cubs and parents at this time is at its peak during daylight hours. Like people, foxes enjoy good weather, and you stand a far greater chance of getting good views if you watch on calm, sunny days.

The ideal for earth observation is one which has very good nearby cover, either a hedgerow or woodland. Earths which are in the middle of open fields or moorland offer few opportunities for the naturalist to cover his or her outline. They do, however, offer a clean line of sight which may help in picking out a returning adult.

Foxes can be watched away from the earth, though not with such predictable results. The best alternative to watching at the breeding den is at a favoured hunting site. This may be a field of pasture, rich with earthworms and small mammals, or perhaps a rabbit warren. Finding such locations is largely a matter of luck, with a bit of applied field craft thrown in.

TRACK AND SIGN

Despite a remarkable ability to remain elusive, foxes do leave quite clear signs of their presence in an area. For the sake of other foxes, territories are marked with urine and dung, as well as copious amounts of scent, produced by glands distributed from many parts of the body. All these signs can be detected by humans and are an invaluable aid to tracking foxes. Other signs include prey remains, hair, footprints, dew paths, snuff holes, etc.

The traditional track—footprints—can be quite tricky to discern. These are similar to a dog's but they do have a couple of characteristic features. First is the shape and size. No fox print is longer than 6 cm, most are a centimetre less, and like a dog they display four toes on each foot. An average-sized dog leaves prints a good 2 cm longer. Domestic dogs leave a rounded print, with the middle toes quite well spaced, and foxes produce an almost diamond-shaped print with the middle toes all but touching, especially at the claws. Unlike badgers, foxes leave few scratch marks during the course of their travels, and on all but the softest ground hardly leave a mark.

Probably the most striking of signs, and certainly the one which most often alerts me that a fox has passed by recently is smell. Each time a fox urinates, and during general locomotion, it produces a very distinctive scent. It is much stronger than that produced by most other wild mammals, with the exception perhaps of rutting deer. If, as you walk through a field or woodland, you catch a sudden whiff of a musky, vaguely aniseed smell, chances are you have picked up the scent of a fox. Usually, you walk straight through the scent trail, but by back–tracking and sniffing, you can almost invariably pick it up again. The scent also has a hint of old wet straw about it, and a hint of body odour. Strange as it may seem, even this smell is not offensive.

Fox scats are another very prolific and noticeable clue. Because part of their function is to mark territory, they are often deposited in the most showy of places: on prominent tufts of grass, stones, bones, logs and on unfinished kills or carrion. Their colour varies from shades of grey to black, but it is their shape which is their most distinctive feature. The best word I can come up with for fox scats is squiggly. Always finely tapered at the end, with many twists and turns in the body of the scat, they look as though they have been squeezed out of an icing bag by an incompetent chef. On close inspection, it can be seen that these twists and tapers are caused by undigested animal hair. Where foxes are living on an urban diet of fish and chips, topped off with bacon rind or any other scraps that are available, the scats take on a much more dog-like appearance. They do, however, retain the tapered end and are more slender and longer than the deposits of most dogs. More usually, scats may contain small mammal hair and crushed bone, beetle chitin, and mud, from eating worms.

Paths or runs are not really a feature useful for tracking foxes, because they tend to use existing clearways or a fairly random, meandering path through the territory. Where they pass beneath fences or gates they may use a favourite spot which can be distinguished by hair deposits, scent, and prints. Fox hair is very fine on the belly, and a combination of fine insulating hair and rather coarser guard hairs on the back. The colours are distinctive—a creamy-white on the belly and a sandy to brick-red on the back. Many of the red guard hairs have a red base, dark centre, and red tip, occasionally finished off with a small amount of creamy-white. The general appearance is fluffy, unlike most dog's thicker hair.

In early morning you might find dew paths. These are formed by anything which has moved through a field of pasture, are very difficult to attribute to a single species, and are created by the feet or body of an animal as it brushes against the grass, so knocking off the dew as it goes. In the correct light, this looks like a dark streak running throughout the pale, wet grass. On a known track, such as a badger's or an otter's, dew paths can tell you that an animal has passed by recently. But with foxes, they often reveal early morning meanderings in search of voles, worms and beetles. Such tracks are always narrow: in long grass they form a constant thread; in short grass, individual foot marks. It is the random pattern which gives the best clue that a fox has made them, but it is wise to substantiate your diagnosis with another clue, such as scent or scats somewhere along the path.

Like badgers, foxes often form snuff holes when searching for worms or grubs, but these tend to be narrower and without such distinctive claw marks. Other signs of feeding are much more unique to foxes, particularly prey remains. When a fox kills a bird, it usually plucks it before feeding. Breast feathers can normally be tugged out with the incisors and often clog up in a sticky mass around the fox's mouth. Periodically, they will be wiped off with a foot, or more normally by rubbing the face and jaw along the ground, leaving tell-tale clumps of breast feathers, stuck together with saliva. Wing feathers are much harder to pluck, and these are normally chewed off with the fox's sharp molar teeth. On a bird the size of a pigeon, several primary feathers will be snipped off together, and each will have a neat cut at the quill.

When a rabbit is killed it is usually eaten completely, but tufts of hair, stuck together with saliva, may, like feathers, be cleaned from the jaw on the ground nearby. Hedgehogs are sometimes killed and eaten, leaving only the spines attached to the skin from the back, like some macabre cape. Mice and voles are bite-sized snacks, and are chewed up in their entirety.

Prey remains littered around a hole are a sure indicator that you have found a fox's breeding earth. I have come across all manner of leftovers, from the front half of a mole, to the back half of a Kentucky Fried Chicken box. The young cubs are not too fussy about where they go to the loo and small foxy droppings are another good sign. Fox earths may be original holes, dug from scratch (no pun intended), or enlarged and reworked rabbit holes. Sometimes a fox family will move into an abandoned section of a badger sett, and I have seen badger cubs and fox cubs playing side by side on more than one occasion. The entrance hole to a fox earth may be quite small, as little as 30 cm across, though the size varies enormously, depending on the hole's original owner. There may be several entrances to an earth, two at least, and nearby excavations may well be the retreat of the adult male or other relative. In some areas of high fox population and good food supply, families may group together to raise one or more litters of cubs.

SENSES

One of the qualities that has made foxes such good survivors in the face of adversity is their unbelievably acute armoury of senses. It is hard to say which is most highly developed. Their hearing is superb, their great parabolas of ears constantly twisting and scanning for the rustle of a mouse or the crunch of a human footstep. A nervous fox, on the lookout for danger, will pick out a human form even if he or she is well camouflaged and perfectly still. The fox's inquisitive nature also makes it a very tough cookie to fool; they are one of the few animals that looks up for danger, so even hiding in trees may not help.

Smell is used the whole time, to pick up the scent of other foxes, find food or evade danger. A fox which is suspicious of an object will often circle downwind to test the air, making it very hard for the human observer to avoid detection.

SOUND ADVICE

Anyone who does not recognize the scream of a fox may easily interpret what they are hearing as the most blood-curdling of human cries. Particularly during winter and the courting period, foxes can set up the most awful din, screeching, wailing, growling and barking. The closest we humans can come to producing a similar sound is in the process of being murdered (not recommended) or by screaming by inhaling rather than exhaling. By trying to produce a falsetto scream as you draw breath you can approximate a fox call.

Another sound very closely associated with the breeding season is the bark. This is quite unlike any dog bark you have ever heard, and in my experience is usually uttered by dog foxes in the height of the mating period in December and January. I have seen it described as the 'wo-wo' bark or the 'rar-rar' bark, both of which are pretty good phonetic labels for this unlikely noise. To produce a sound like it yourself, try saying; 'Rar-rar-rar', whilst inhaling in a high-pitched voice. 'Rar-rar' calls may develop into a screaming session at any time, the barks slowly sliding into a series of high-pitched screeches. Adult foxes may produce a screaming call at any time of year. This is a call based on the same sounds produced when they make their 'murder' screams, but is more regular and evenly spaced. It is quite common to hear five or six screams, with roughly three seconds between each, during the course of the night.

All of the above calls are produced during the hours of darkness. Rarely, if ever, do foxes vocalize very much during the day. There are two common exceptions to this: the warning scream and the calls made by the cubs. The warning scream may be uttered by any fox, though I have heard it most often when a vixen has detected danger whilst she is looking after young. It sounds very like the screaming call described earlier, but is less regularly spaced and often a little quieter. Cubs at play make a wide variety of sounds based on cackles and yelps. The cackling calls are reminiscent of someone trying to clear a fish bone from the back of their throat, and the yelps are like a shortened, more warbling juvenile version of the adult scream.

There are one or two low-volume calls that foxes make which can only be heard if you are very close to the animal. One I describe as the 'uncertain' call. It is produced with the mouth closed from somewhere in the throat and is often linked with the animal coming across a new phenomenon. It even sounds questioning to our ears, a low, growling whine which ascends at the end and lasts no more than one second. A fox which feels seriously threatened and is cornered produces guttural cackles with its mouth open, like a deeper, harsher version of the 'fish-bone' call.

Foxes move very quietly through the woodland or field, much more so than a badger. Occasionally you may hear one scuffing through dead leaves or trotting through a glade, but I have never found these mechanical sounds a particularly good aid to identification. These animals do have a marked effect on many of their neighbours, and may be located by various mobbing calls. Wrens, blackbirds, chaffinches, squirrels and many others will pester a resting fox with their warning cries. A chattering magpie, constantly looking at the ground, may give a very good clue to the whereabouts of a sleeping fox or even a litter of cubs.

OBSERVATION

Watching foxes, especially at the breeding earth, can be tricky because a nervous animal may well react badly if it knows it has been discovered. The first thing to remember if you think you have discovered a breeding earth is never to walk up to the hole and look down it. Nine times out of ten this would have little or no effect on the inhabitants, but one in ten the fox is so nervous that even the smell of a human being across the earth is enough to make them abandon the site. Vixens will very readily move their cubs to a new location. Always check holes from a distance of at least 3 metres, more if possible. Once you think you have found an active earth, retreat and find a good hiding spot as far away as possible, still keeping a clear view of the holes and surrounding area. This distant watch is very important. It enables you to monitor the most frequent direction used by the adult foxes when they leave and arrive at the earth without frightening them, and this knowledge is essential if you want to find a suitable place to hide a bit closer. Arrive at your distant observation point early and stay late. Pick a dry, preferably sunny, wind-free day. Carefully note the direction from which any adult fox arrives, and any leaving the earth. Note, too, the wind direction and time of day with each adult movement. It is worth keeping a record of the times cubs emerge, though at the height of their diurnal activity, they can spring out at virtually any moment. I normally continue distant observations for at least two days.

With a good knowledge of the fox family timetable, you are ready to take a closer look. Always remember that if you are discovered by the vixen, you may never see the fox cubs in the same location again, as well as causing unnecessary stress to the family. Don't be tempted to go too close at this stage; despite the young cubs being fairly immune when it comes to human disturbance the adults are not, and a distance of 9 to 15 metres is a reasonable range. Look for available natural cover: a hedgerow, a stand of trees, or bracken are all good. Make sure that they are away from all of the usual adult approach routes and that they are downwind of the site. Sometimes it is enough to settle behind or in front of these natural screens, but more usually you will have to make some extra cover. When building a hide or screen, use available material or scrim. The use of a canvas hide standing out in the open may be too great a change of scenery for some foxes.

If you have pale skin exposed, cover it, and wear silent, well camouflaged clothing. Approach the earth with caution because the dog or vixen may be lying up nearby, and may be frightened by your arrival. If you do see an adult fox run from the site, or hear a warning scream, continue to walk straight on and leave the site altogether for at least an hour. This should convince the adult foxes that your presence was entirely accidental. If the cubs are up and playing when you arrive to watch, it should be possible for you to reach your close observation point without too much difficulty. The reaction of young foxes to a human being varies greatly according to their age and individual character. When first above ground, as small, brown, bear-like cubs, they have very poor eyesight. It may be possible to walk right up to them, even touch them with no apparent ill effects. But however lost and lonely they may look, never attempt to get too close or handle the cubs. Every year, thousands of young foxes are handed in to the RSPCA and wildlife rescue centres around the country, by well meaning but ill informed people. It is all too easy to think that the cute little bundles of fur are orphaned when in fact the only thing keeping their mother away is you. As the cubs get older they get increasingly wary, and at six to eight weeks of age they may become nervous if they see you enter a hiding place.

When observing adult foxes, pay special attention to their ears and the direction of their gaze. Even a completely relaxed animal, with apparently sleepy eyes, will disappear in a flash if it spots you moving. A fox facing 180 degrees away from you may have its ears twisted back and be listening to your every move. If you are discovered, allow things to settle before quietly and quickly leaving the site. If you plan to re-visit, allow a day or two's rest, and start by making a long-distance observation again. You may find that even though remaining at the earth, the foxes have become cautious of your old hiding place and it is a shrewd move for you to find a new one.

When you wish to leave an earth that you have been watching, do so only once the whole family has gone underground or off hunting. The habit some dog foxes and vixens have of sitting above ground, keeping a lookout, can make for some very long waits.

Though hunting by day is not uncommon, foxes are much more active during the night. Many foxes react very badly to torchlight, almost certainly as a result of people dazzling them with lamps when trying to shoot them. Away from the earth it is certainly possible to attract inexperienced foxes to within a metre or so, by shining a light on them and producing a sound like a mouse's squeak or a rabbit scream.

A more rewarding way of attracting foxes at night, and throughout the day, can be achieved during the courting period. By mimicking the 'rar-rar' bark, it is sometimes possible to attract several lusty animals to within a few metres, and to observe the interaction between them. When mimicking a bark, don't overdo it; you are far more likely to bring the animals close to you if you bark infrequently. When they do get close, it's best if you keep quiet and still, and having observed them, allow them to go about their business with no further duping.

It is possible to habituate foxes but to get a wary, rural fox used to you takes an enormous amount of time, and the animal may never truly settle. I have met one or two exceptional creatures whose nature was such that I worried for their ultimate survival in a land so full of enemies. One litter of six cubs I filmed, which were raised amongst a pile of hay bales, included one I shall never forget. At first I approached the filming as I would for any other fox litter, using great caution and being well concealed. Imagine my amazement when one evening this eight-week old cub walked straight up to my hiding place, sniffed my feet, and instead of bolting for cover sat down and stared at me. Over the following days and weeks, we played chase, tug of war (with a goose feather and a crisp packet), and general rough and tumble. I watched the earth for the whole summer, and though I saw the other cubs and the adults often, I always had to treat them with as much caution as I would any other wild fox. Towards the end of the summer, when the cubs started wandering further afield, I grew worried that my russet friend would fall prey to the first hostile human being he met. Though it went against the grain, I started trying to scare him each time he came up to me, and little by little he became more wary. He was never truly nervous of humans though, and his trust may well have sealed his fate.

Foxes can be watched hunting by using several different techniques. The first, and in my experience the most successful, is to hide close to a likely source of prey, such as a rabbit warren. Use all the concealment and observation methods you would employ to watch an earth, and pick a location where you have a good field of view over a wide area, with little ground vegetation to obstruct your line of sight. I have observed hunting at all times of year but have been best rewarded during the months when hungry litters of cubs are being cared for. I have also filmed hunting foxes from a car, driving along quiet lanes until I spot an animal, and using the car as a hide. Foxes differ enormously in their reaction to cars, and the only way you will know if this method works in your area is to try it out.

City foxes require completely different tactics. Because we are predominantly active by day, they tend to be active by night. Young cubs will play around a quiet earth during daylight, but most foraging occurs after midnight. The best urban areas I have found for fox watching all have some reasonably large tract of natural cover nearby, such as a park or a series of large gardens. The time to watch is usually from midnight through to about 5 am, and because of the street lighting in most cities, this nocturnal vigil can produce some very clear, if very orange views. Any dustbin within walking distance of a fast-food take-away will be a favourite hunting ground, as will the gardens and rubbish of houses within the territory. Driving slowly around town, trying to spot foxes, may result in embarrassing moments with the local constabulary, so it often pays to let them know what you plan to do, and the registration of your vehicle the day before. The car is, in fact, one of the best hides for watching urban foxes, because it represents nothing more than scenery to them. They may get a little nervous if you stop the vehicle, but should settle soon after.

PHOTOGRAPHY

You are armed with a camera and long focal length lens; they are armed with ears that will pick up the sound of a shutter being released as though it were a rifle shot, and eyes that spot every glint and glare from a lens, every twitch and twist of a hand on the focus ring. To acclimatize foxes to lens shine, I often leave a dummy sticking out of an observation screen and this seems to settle all but the jumpiest of animals. Good lens hoods also help reduce reflection and improve your photographs by eliminating flare. I camouflage all of my camera equipment using a self-adhesive tape, designed for camouflaging guns and bows. As well as helping to reduce reflections from shiny anodized surfaces, this also helps to give your kit a bit of bush cred.

Noisy camera shutters, motor winds, and any other clicks and bumps are a real problem with most foxes. The most effective way of 'blimping' these sounds is to use layers of thick coats or other insulating fabric over the camera, lens, and if need be, yourself. I have fiddled around trying to make good blimps which cover only the stills camera and still leave all of the operational controls to hand, but the fact is none has been as effective at reducing noise as the coat and blanket method. If, after you have taken a photo, the fox looks in your direction, wait until it relaxes and looks away before taking any more. After a few shots you should find that you are being ignored. The coat and blanket method of sound insulation also helps to guard against your movements catching the eye of your subject, because the fabric can be draped completely over your head and hands to allow focusing, change of shutter speed and any other operation to be carried out unseen.

Many of the same problems which face a stills photographer also apply to anyone wishing to take cine film or video. The same remedies can be applied, but any equipment used for capturing a moving image is likely to be quite bulky, and this will have to be considered when choosing a hiding place. Both cine and stills can be taken at night using methods similar to those described for badgers. I have found that urban foxes take quite readily to a constant artificial light, but have never tried to do the same with rural animals. I have seen foxes many times whilst I have been waiting at an artificially lit badger sett, and they have almost invariably hung around the edges of the light. Whether this was due to the lights or due to their reluctance to walk straight into the heart of badger territory, I do not know. Flash photography with foxes can be quite successful, again using methods similar to those used with badgers. The biggest differences are that foxes are far more wary, and much less predictable in their movements around the territory, so presenting a challenge with remote set-ups.

The Deer
(Cervidae)

Of the five species of deer found commonly across Britain and Europe, many share similar traits and habits. There is enough difference between them, however, to warrant separate headings for each. I have consciously omitted Chinese water deer and reindeer, as both are feral and unlikely to be encountered over most of the British Isles.

Roe Deer
(Capreolus capreolus)

Of all the deer species likely to be seen in Britain and Europe, roe is certainly the most widespread. It is a creature ideally suited to a temperate climate, unlike some of its introduced cousins, and as such has colonized almost every suitable habitat. But despite its success and proliferation, it is rarely seen. This is testament to its shy, retiring nature, and remarkable ability to remain undetected in relatively little cover. If I had to pick a favourite deer species, this would be it. It is shy, nimble, sometimes fiery, and always utterly lovely to watch.

WHERE AND WHEN

This species is found over much of Europe, and in the UK, is widespread. Roe can be seen from the Scottish highlands to the New Forest, from Cornwall to Suffolk. In all these locations they frequent a wide variety of habitats; in Wiltshire, for example, they use the wide open plains and wheat fields so typical of the region; in Somerset or Hampshire they tend to be creatures of woodland, hedgerow and forest. It is their liking for wooded areas that has created something of a confrontation between the deer and forestry concerns, because roe frequently fray the bark from young trees with their antlers and nibble the tops off many others.

Their calendar is unusual amongst British deer, because the rut occurs in the summer and not the autumn. The last week of July, first week of August are the best times to watch roe rutting, though I have often heard of a second or false rut occurring later in October. I have seen bucks chasing does during this period, but I have never seen them successfully mount, whereas chases in the summer are generally consummated. Male and female deer have certain key events which govern the course of their year. For the males these events all revolve around keeping a territory and mating, the female's routine is governed more by the birth and raising of their young.

After the summer rut, the male deer relax a little bit and often become much less conspicuous, resting and recuperating after the rigours of the breeding season. Unlike some other deer species, they do not usually form bachelor herds, but remain within their territory and continue to defend it against other adult male deer. As winter approaches, the bucks start to lose their antlers and regrow a new set. Like all deer, mature animals usually grow larger, more impressive antlers. These remain in velvet, the soft fluffy skin which covers them, during the course of their

growth until early spring when the hormone testosterone again starts to flow around the buck's body, inhibiting the growth of the antler and hardening it. It is then, during March and April, that most bucks clean the dead velvet from their antlers and begin their serious territorial defences once again. Younger bucks lose their antlers and velvet later than older ones, and I have seen many yearling males in 'tatters', the period when the velvet is being lost, during late April or even May.

Now that the mature bucks are fully equipped to deal with any dispute which may occur with the neighbours, they begin to mark their territory by fraying, scent-marking and occasionally barking. They also chase any subordinate males from their territory and fight with any which match their strength and tenacity. Fights can occur at any time during the spring and summer, though most that I have seen have taken place during the early stages of territorial confirmation. As the spring develops, the deer start to loose their grey-brown winter coats and adopt the beautiful deep russet of their summer pelage. Also at this time of year, a short period during April and early May, those which inhabit woodland spend a good deal of time grazing in nearby open fields. This feeding behaviour may well occur as a result of fresh grass and broad leaf herb growth, ahead of the leaves on shrubs and bushes. Once the bramble, hazel and others start to unfurl their green bounty, the deer adopt much more of a browsing style of feeding, though they will graze on occasion throughout the year, and depending on habitat, may rely on ground vegetation for much of their diet. As July approaches, the bucks get revved up again in preparation for the rut and indulge in much fraying, barking, chasing and fighting.

The female's year is much more sedate. After the rut, the embryo does not begin developing immediately, but is held in suspension until the spring. This is the only species of deer in the British Isles which displays delayed implantation. By October, the winter coat is growing well, and with the onset of autumn, many deer start to forage in the open. Also at this time, any young from the summer which are still with their mothers are encouraged to leave, the doe making repeated charges at them. Young males are less likely to be around at this time than females, because they will have been discouraged already by the dominant buck during the rut. Even in midwinter, however, it is not uncommon to see small family groups of three or four roe all feeding together. Females play a very passive role during the spring, feeding well now that the embryo within has started to develop.

Roe kids are usually born in late May, early June, and it is the norm for does to give birth to twins, sometimes even triplets. Roe deer, like most other creatures are very secretive whilst giving birth, and for a short time in the spring and summer seem to disappear from the countryside. Once the kids are born, often in long grass or thick shrubby cover, their mother leaves them for long periods between feeds. At this time they are very vulnerable, their only defence a magnificent camouflage and ability to remain perfectly still. It is the combination of an absentee mother and apparently weak, defenceless kid, which leads many people to believe that they have discovered an orphan, and pick it up to take it into care. Sadly, once this is done the youngster has a very small chance of survival and unless returned very quickly to its hiding place will indeed be an orphan. Even the act of handling the baby, covering it in human scent, may be enough to convince a highly-strung doe that any return to nurse her offspring would be too great a risk.

As soon as they are fully mobile, roughly one week after birth, the kids start to follow their mother around wherever she goes. During late evening in the early summer, the kids often cavort and gamble in lunatic bouts of play, and their high spirits are often infectious enough to get their mother involved in the game. Roe does and kids rarely gang up to form collective groups at this time of year, preferring instead to keep a healthy distance between themselves and any neighbouring family. They are, however, quite likely to tolerate the presence of the dominant buck. As the rut approaches, the does begin to leave frequent urine marks and may begin to call from time to time as they come into season.

The best habitat for watching roe deer is wooded country interspersed with frequent open spaces. This sort of ground provides you with ample hiding places coupled with clear views. Deer which use open plains are usually much harder to approach, and those in thick woodland or forest are only ever in sight for brief periods. Sometimes gardens are raided for their tasty morsels; roe seem to have a particular passion for roses. This trait has earned the deer such a reputation in some southern areas that roe-proof varieties of rose have been developed.

The daily routine of these deer differs with habitat, disturbance level, time of month and season. In areas where they are not persecuted they are just as likely to be active by day as by night. Early morning and late evening are always the busiest times of day, and when a buck is marking territory, he will often do the rounds at about midday. During the full moon, deer tend to feed much more by night, though even this doesn't prevent diurnal activity during the rut.

TRACK AND SIGN

Of all the European species of deer, roe leave some of the most distinctive and unique signs. They come in the form of droppings, tracks, runs, rings, lies, scrapes and fraying stocks. Roe droppings are usually found in collected heaps along runs or more often next to lies. They are small, dark brown or black pellets, not much bigger than a rabbit dropping, cylindrical in shape, and pointed at one end, sometimes slightly concave at the other. Sheep dung is usually scattered much more randomly and has a less well defined bullet shape. Roe deer and sheep, however, do not usually mix: I have never seen roe happily grazing alongside sheep flocks, and fields which have been grazed by sheep seem to be avoided by the deer for some time after the last one has been removed. Roe will happily graze alongside cattle and horses.

Roe tracks often show well, even on quite hard soils. The whole slot or print of an adult buck is about the length of a man's thumb, and 2.5–3 cm wide at the base. The does leave a slightly smaller mark. Being cloven hoofed, the space between the two toes alters according to the surface and speed at which the animal is travelling. On soft ground the toes are spread, as they may be if the deer is turning sharply or leaping. On hard ground and at a walking pace, the toe tips are kept close together, forming a tear-drop shaped print. The most likely track to

Above: Roe deer may often be seen browsing or resting on the edge of pasture. Females and their young stay together for much of the year.

Above: A hide set up for filming nesting herring gulls on Steep Holm Island. The birds here became so used to the hides, they often perched on the roof.

Opposite, above left: A well-used otters' sprainting point on the Scottish west coast. The white, crumbly spraints are old; the black ones more recent.

Opposite, above right: Runs like this are often found where otters take a short cut across a headland, and usually have spraint deposited somewhere along their length.

Opposite, below left: This dung pit has recently been used by several different badgers and reveals the diversity of dung forms according to the animals' last meal.

Opposite, below right: The bottom strand of a barbed wire fence is a good place to search for badger hair.

cause confusion is that of a sheep, but the latter have broader heels to the foot, a wider gap from back to front between the two toes, and a comparatively blunt tip. Roe slots look neat and sleek by comparison. On very hard ground, it is often just the tip of the hoof which leaves a mark, looking like two 'V' shapes, side by side.

Roe runs or paths are most noticeable in woodland. Sometimes the deer adopt an existing clearway, either human or badger, but they also create their own. Unless very well used, or shared by other species, roe runs are not usually very clear of debris. Often they are littered with dead leaves which do not appear to be well flattened, and this untidy appearance is caused by the animal's neat footed, high stepping gait. The exception to this can be found where the deer leap across gullies or scrabble up slopes, as here they wear the ground back to bare soil, covered with the toe marks and scratches from their hooves. The run is usually quite wide, at least 13 cm, and where it passes through dense cover, such as blackthorn or bramble, leaves a tunnel about 50 to 60 cm high, much higher than most badger, fox or otter runs.

It is always worth carefully checking runs for hair, especially through thick cover or a wire fence. The dark winter hair is shed in April and May and can sometimes be found in great clumps. It is very distinctive, more because of shape than colour, as it is heavily corrugated. It is coarse, dark grey or brown in the main part, with a paler base and tip, and the corrugations are most pronounced towards the tip (the rare and very local Chinese water deer also has corrugations on its hair, but these are less obvious and the hair is much thicker and paler than a roe's). The summer coat is sometimes tugged loose as the deer pass through barbed wire fences and is usually found on the second or third strand from the ground. It is also fairly coarse, but reddish-brown in colour, and the corrugations are less well pronounced or completely absent.

Left: Many eider duck will sit very tight on the nest, allowing the careful observer to approach to within a metre or so.

From March to August, male deer leave many signs for others of their species to read, and these aid the human tracker a great deal. When the velvet is being cleaned from the antlers in March and April, it is possible to find strips of the shed skin left on or around fraying stocks. Sometimes the deer, particularly young males, will use any bush, small tree or shrub to rid themselves of the redundant skin, but the more mature animals may well start to use specific trees or bushes for the job. As the antlers become clean, these same trees are often used to leave scent marks, and they become very worn in the process.

From my own observations, a mature buck typically frays less often and on thicker, more mature trees and shrubs than a younger animal. A yearling buck, for example, may walk through a hazel coppice, stopping every 15 metres or so to rub his new antlers against anything within reach. A mature buck, by comparison, will have specific, prominent trees within and around the boundary of his territory, and will visit each in turn to fray and leave a scent mark from the glands between the antlers and below the eye. I have never been able to clearly smell roe deer at any time of year.

Most fraying stocks, be they young deciduous trees, conifers, or shrubs, measure no more than 6 or 8 cm in diameter, and are often much smaller. Fraying in young conifer plantations can badly damage the trees, though the activities of a single dominant buck are nowhere near as brutal as those from several young males. It may be that where a dominant buck has died, it makes room for a greater number of vigorous youngsters, all disputing the territorial rights, and creating pro-portionately much more damage than the older animal.

A fraying stock can be recognized by an area on the tree which is free of small branches, and has most or all of the bark frayed off, leaving ragged, often hanging strips of bark above and below the fray-line. Such bare areas are often concentrated on one side of the tree, and are between 0.75 to 1 metre, above the ground. The band of exposed trunk is rarely more than 20 or 30 cm from top to bottom.

At the base of the most actively used fraying stocks, the male deer often make scrapes. These form a fan shape in the soil, the narrowest point of which is nearest the tree, and are often completely clear of leaf litter. They vary a great deal in size, from about 30 cm long to over 1 metre on the most vigorously used sites. Because the roe is equipped with scent glands in the feet, these scrapes almost certainly represent another pungent message to passers-by that the territory is occupied. I have also seen bucks urinate on them from time to time.

Both sexes, and all ages will also make scrapes or lies, to rest in. These are areas, often within a few metres of a run and in some form of cover, where the animal scrapes and turns around on the ground in the same manner as a dog making a bed, before lying down to rest and ruminate. Such lies often have a pile of droppings on the edge of them, and it is common to find two or three together, indicating that a family has rested together. They are often quite a large oval shape, at least 1 to 1.5 metres long.

During the rut, the male deer often pursue the does in small circles or figures of eight, and this behaviour gives rise to roe rings. The repeated circling quickly wears the ground into remarkably clear paths that follow the course, and to the casual observer they are apparently useless footpaths that never reach a destination. In woodland or shrubby country, they are often formed around a bush or a tree, but they do occur in open fields and are less well defined here.

Roe deer browse in a fairly random manner, nibbling a bramble bush here, a hazel bud there. In winter, they sometimes chew the tops off young conifers, but then so do most other deer species. This makes it very hard to identify a roe deer by its feeding signs alone.

SENSES

To say a roe deer has a good sense of hearing is the same as saying that Mount Everest is quite big. Basically, they have brilliant hearing which presents something of a challenge to the field naturalist. Their sense of smell is also acute, and their eyesight is pretty good, too.

Roe are always on the edge of running; every step they take seems to be full of tension and the slightest unusual sound is picked up by their great, radar ears. They are also prone to move downwind of an unidentified object they have spotted and can pick up human scent over a tremendous distance.

They are not adept at spotting an inanimate form that is reasonably camouflaged, and under the right conditions, may come very close before sensing anything untoward.

SOUND ADVICE

Roe are probably the least vocal of all the British deer, but nonetheless produce some distinctive calls and mechanical sounds. The call you are most likely to hear is an alarm bark, usually produced when an animal has smelled or heard a perceived threat. It closely resembles a single bark of a large dog, is deep and explosive in quality, and often signifies that the deer, though anxious, is not entirely convinced of the identity of the danger. Just because you hear the sound, this does not mean all is lost. Phonetically, the sound is 'boff'. Sometimes more than one bark is made, especially when the deer is on the move, each subsequent call, quieter and quicker than the first, something like 'BOFF ... BOf ... Bof ... bof .. bof. Both sexes produce this sound, an adult male's call is significantly deeper than a female's.

The bucks sometimes produce a very similar call when they are vigorously declaring territory. Generally, territorial barking occurs between April and July, is delivered in short bouts and cannot be attributed to any known disturbance. Adult bucks can be 'called up' by imitating the bark during the spring and summer, though you have to be careful not to sound too threatening. The bigger, stronger bucks often have deeper tones, and if you sound dangerously fit your calls may be enough to convince any potential opponents that discretion is the better part of valour.

The bucks also make several much more quiet sounds, or at least they are quiet to our ears. When moving excitedly through their territory, they sometimes make a thin, reedy wheezing call, like someone trying to whistle with a bit of grass between their thumbs. This same quality of sound is produced during chases, though in a much more frequent and excited manner.

The females are very quiet throughout the year. The only time they call is when they are trying to locate one of their offspring, and during the rut. Both calls are similar—a thin, high-pitched whistle, again with a reedy quality. They are usually delivered well spaced, at least ten seconds between calls and with long gaps between bouts of calling. Deer stalkers have traditionally used specially designed whistles to imitate the call of the roe doe. Used properly during the rut, the sound is an irresistible (and sometimes fatal) attraction to the bucks who come running to the source of the sound. As a means of observing natural behaviour, mimicking the doe call has limitations, because all the buck is likely to do once he has reached you is sniff around for a while before charging off after more fruitful encounters. The kids produce a whistle when they are lost, which is a higher, thinner version of the doe call.

The only other vocalization I have heard about, though never experienced first-hand, is a scream produced when the animal is extremely stressed. Produced by male and female alike, I have heard it described as a shrill, reedy whistle, very loud, and not unlike a deep rabbit squeal.

A roe moving through woodland makes a very distinctive sound in the leaf litter and undergrowth. Assuming you know that no other deer species inhabit the place you are watching, there are no other creatures which produce the same, hesitant foot-falls as this. The rhythm approximates that of a small horse, interspersed with many pauses and missed beats. If a deer senses you and is certain of your identity, it will run using very pronounced, prancing leaps which fall very heavily on the ground. I have often startled deer when making my way through dense woodland, and had cause to wonder which of us was the most alarmed. The sound of this dash for safety is really quite explosive at close quarters. It is, of course, a clear sign to other deer that something is up, and one deer running in this manner often has the effect of alerting others to your presence. Unlike some other deer species, I have never seen a roe truly 'pronk' or 'stott', a sort of stiff-legged run where the deer leaps into the air using all four legs at the same time.

When a roe is running, it is sometimes possible to hear a clicking sound. This comes from the cloven hooves springing together each time they leave the ground, and is a noise I do not associate with any other deer species.

OBSERVATION

Roe are very much creatures of habit, and, if undisturbed, may walk at the same times to the same places every day. This helps the field naturalist when it comes to picking the right spot for a good view. Just where this is changes with the seasons, and can vary, from the heart of the wood to the fields surrounding it.

Roe often come on to pasture during the spring and this is a good time for watching. Find out which fields the deer are using. This is best done from a distance, either using a car, or by carefully walking along the inside edge of a wood. Pick the hour of last light to make these preliminary observations. If you choose to walk, pick a route which prevents your scent passing ahead of you on the breeze. If, during your passage through the habitat, you encounter any deer, do not stop to look at them. If anything, you should avoid looking straight in their direction at all, as deer, in common with many other animals, will remain perfectly still so long as they believe they have gone unnoticed. It is possible to walk to within a few metres of a roe in thick cover, so long as you avoid turning to face it, pausing or altering the line of your progress. It is a sobering thought that for every deer I have spotted in this way, I must have blindly walked straight past many more.

Having established where the deer are feeding, you have the option of stalking them, or lying in wait. Both methods work equally well under certain conditions. I prefer to use the wait-and-see method most of the time because it holds the smallest risk of disturbing the animals and often presents the most prolonged views of relaxed, natural behaviour.

Roe deer are very nervous during high winds, and are none too happy about leaving the shelter of the woods in rain storms. Like so many creatures, they enjoy a bit of sunshine on their back and can be particularly active by day if the nights have been dark (no moon) and wet. Choose your hiding place carefully, making sure you know where the deer emerge from the woodland on to the field, and which way they generally move whilst grazing. Look for some available cover which you can use to hide your outline, perhaps some bushes or trees which afford a good clear view and which are downwind of the main area of activity. I usually use scrim and available vegetation to build a small observation screen in front of my hiding place, leaving just my head, fully camouflaged, poking above it.

Arrive at the site at least two hours before sunset and settle quickly. Keep a constant eye out for deer on the edge of the wood and any lying down on the field borders; often the only part of the animal that shows up in dense cover is its pale rump, so be particularly vigilant for any white or cream shapes. As they start to arrive on the field to feed, allow them to settle before moving a muscle. As with most animals, keep perfectly still and quiet as if you are being watched. Roe sometimes pretend to feed when in fact they are listening and looking at you. Make sure they are genuinely chewing, and not just sniffing the ground before you raise your binoculars or make any other move.

A more elaborate form of deer observation, often employed by professional deer stalkers, involves the use of a high seat. This structure works on the principle that deer do not usually look up for danger. Assuming you remain quiet and relatively still, a high seat can provide fantastically close views of the animals, sometimes passing directly beneath you. The simplest variety is nothing more than a plank in a tree, which gives you somewhere relatively comfortable to perch whilst you wait. I have also used portable seats which strap on to trees, lightweight metal seats complete with ladders, and the more permanent wooden structures which resemble little towers. Anything which puts you more than 3 metres above the ground will do the job, and all designs benefit through being attached or close to an existing tree. An isolated, free-standing high seat may well attract attention, both from the deer and from human passers-by. The position of a high seat is very important, whether in woodland or on the edge of a clearing. I usually ensure that at least two are available to overlook an area, allowing for various wind conditions. Sometimes, a seat erected close to a well-used deer path will provide excellent, if brief, views of the animals. Despite the roe deer's tendency to concentrate on dangers from the ground, they will look up if they spot a movement or hear a strange sound and so it is important, even in a high seat, to keep still and quiet at all times.

Much of the roe deer's behaviour occurs whilst the animal is on the move, and a stalking method of observation may sometimes be more rewarding. Use the camouflage and walking methods described in Section 1 of this book, with special emphasis on silent movement and wind monitoring. It often pays to clear some woodland paths of noisy sticks and dead leaves a day or two before you intend to move through the area.

Adult male deer are often much harder to watch than the females, and this probably has something to do with their attracting more attention from human hunters who are looking for the antlers as a trophy. The bucks are often the last to come out to feed in the evening and the first to disappear back into the woods in the morning.

PHOTOGRAPHY

When trying to get photographs of roe deer, you face a constant battle with sound. The slightest click, rustle or knock is enough to send most dashing for cover, which can make lens changing, film winding and shutter release a real headache. I generally prefer to use manual film advance with deer that are within close range, having found that the prolonged whine of most motor drives is too noisy for most. I also insulate the sound the camera makes by draping fabric over the camera body, lens and sometimes my head.

I would expect to use a long focal length lens, of at least 300 mm, that is capable of working in low light levels. Though there is always a temptation to use a high speed film with an animal which is so likely to be active in poor light, the results on anything over 200 ASA are always a grainy disappointment. I tend to stick to 64 or 50 ASA slide film, regardless of conditions, telling myself that anything that is too dark to photograph with these high definition emulsions, is not worth photographing anyway.

Use of a high seat or ground-level screen as described in the Observation section are both good strategies for photographing more relaxed deer behaviour. This is especially true if you want to record a moving image with video or film, as there is nothing worse than a series of shots which have the animals looking straight at camera then bolting off into the distance.

Red Deer

(Cervus elaphus)

The largest land mammal in Britain, and surely one of the most magnificent symbols of the wilderness, red deer have, for generations, captured the imagination like no other creature. Their scale and grandeur have attracted mankind, from the most primitive hunter gatherers, as a source of tools honed from their antlers and as food, to the aesthetes who enjoy an ornamental deer herd, grazing on the lawn of a stately home. These are the deer most people are likely to have contact with, whether on a bleak Scottish hill, a park in the south of England, or in a farmed enclosure, kept for the value of their meat. But however domestic the environment, there is something irrepressible about the wild spirit which smoulders just behind their eyes.

WHERE AND WHEN

A big animal like this needs big country if it is going to survive. Wild red deer are animals of forest, hill and moorland. They are traditionally an animal of open mixed forest, grazing and browsing on a wide variety of plant types. As most of the native forest has been destroyed in Europe, they have become more an animal of the open moor, the last wide spaces where their numbers can find any sanctuary. In the UK, red deer are found in good numbers on Exmoor and the Quantocks; a small population still persists in the New Forest in Hampshire, and apart from these isolated groups, the next big stronghold is in the Scottish highlands. They do turn up from time to time in quite unlikely places, but most of these wanderers can be attributed to escapees from the many parks and farms around the country.

The fact that this species is so popular with ornamental parks makes it an ideal candidate for the inexperienced field naturalist for honing his or her observational or photographic skills. Probably the most famous deer park in the country, the Royal Park at Richmond, harbours some of the most magnificent stags that I have ever seen. Though these managed collections of deer offer wonderful opportunities for close, unhurried views of the species, they do not challenge the skills of the devoted field naturalist for whom the thrill has as much to do with the setting and the problems associated with achieving a good view, as the quality of the view itself.

Each habitat occupied by red deer presents a different technique for observation. On Exmoor, the deer seem to favour the wooded valleys, bordered by fields of pasture and, unfortunately for them, the kale and beet which is grown as a winter feed for cattle. In the New Forest, the red deer spend a lot of time on privately owned estates which offer lush grazing and wooded cover, but many return to traditional rutting areas of open heathland bordered by forest. The Scottish deer occupy all manner of habitats, from the high moors and hills in summer, to the lowland pastures in winter. They also browse on fresh young conifer tops in forestry plantations throughout the year.

Red deer follow a pretty strict calendar, and like the roe deer, this differs tremendously between the males and females. The female or hind move away from the herd to give birth to a single calf around May or June, and as soon as the youngster is fully mobile, rejoin the all-female group, which may consist of several relatives; daughters, sisters, aunts, etc. At this time, the herd will be using the area which offers the best feed as well as the greatest protection from danger, which, in the UK, is humans for the adults, and for the very young calves, foxes and golden eagles.

As the summer progresses the young deer often indulge in crazy play sessions, particularly during fine evenings. With the approach of autumn comes the rut, when male and female alike move towards traditionally used areas for mating. The hind seem to respond to the roaring of the stags and may visit a rutting area for a few days, mate, then move away to re-form a female herd. Later in the winter, these herds may be joined by one or two adult males, but generally they remain predominantly single sexed. In the hardest weather the deer living in hilly areas may move down to feed in the relative comfort of the valleys and lowlands. At all times, but particularly in winter when disputes over the best food break out, female red deer may box, rearing up on their back legs and kicking out with their fore feet. Such battles are usually very short-lived.

In common with most deer, the males face a pretty lazy year apart for the concentrated period of activity during the rut. In March or April, they cast their antlers (one old stag I knew dropped his antlers on or about 15 March every year for eight years). Despite forming 'bachelor' herds, the stags usually move away from the other males when they are about to cast their old antlers, and my guess is this serves as a method of self-preservation (see the section on Fallow Deer). With the antlers lost, the bachelor herd re-forms and feeds well through the summer months, resulting in pot bellies and antler growth. The antlers remain in velvet until late August, early September when most disputes are settled with bouts of boxing. Then a remarkable physiological and behavioural change takes place. As the velvet is frayed from the stag's new weapons, the once peaceable group of males now turns into a gang of arch rivals. The younger stags start to spar and quarrel as the more mature animals begin to gravitate towards the rutting areas.

These mature animals develop massive neck strength, slim waists and find their voice. The peak of the red deer rut is usually in late September, early October, though this differs widely according to the location. If I had to pick a date to watch the rut, it would be around 10 October, but weather conditions make a huge difference to the amount of activity. A hard frost, followed by a beautiful clear, crisp, wind-free dawn are undeniably the best conditions for bringing the rutting stags into the peak of their fervour. By the end of October, the rut is petering out and the exhausted stags slowly move away from the stands to feed again in the forests and lowlands with winter threatening lean times to come. Bit by bit, they re-form bachelor herds, though some occasionally join up with the females for a short while through the winter.

TRACK AND SIGN

Given that they are such big animals, you wouldn't think that red deer would be hard to track down. Wrong. They can be among the most elusive of creatures, ducking and weaving like shadows, one step ahead of the observer, leaving in their wake a number of signs letting you know how tantalizingly close you have been. The most obvious of these is their slot. These are the largest cloven hoof prints likely to be encountered in Britain, with the exception of the rare and very local reindeer and the much larger cattle. They follow all the characteristics of most deer prints (see Roe Deer, Track and Sign), but are easily distinguished by their scale and depth. A big stag will have a slot measuring at least 8 or 9 cm from base to tip. They are rather more rounded at the base than those of a roe deer or fallow deer, and because of the herding nature of the animal, are usually found in numerous, trampled, indistinct masses. The droppings vary according to the food supply or the time of year. Most that I have found in summer have been black, of a similar shape to a roe deer dropping, but considerably larger and more randomly scattered. Sometimes, especially in winter, the individual droppings hold together in a cluster. At this time, too, it is common to find much looser dung, resembling a small cow pat.

Red deer, like other deer, will use traditional runs to and from favoured feeding areas, and these are best distinguished by the presence of slots and dung found along the way. Despite the animal's size, these runs are often not much wider than anything made by a badger or a roe deer, so dainty are they on their feet. Where the deer push through thick cover or fences, it is not uncommon to find hair. The moult from the dark brown winter coat into the red summer coat occurs in the spring, from March through April, and this is naturally when most hairy clues can be found. Red deer hair is slightly corrugated and is very thick and coarse. The winter pelage is pale brown at the base, almost black in the middle, and pale red-brown towards the tip, sometimes with a dark point. The summer coat is a pretty consistent red-brown throughout, though more coarse, much longer and straighter than a roe deer's.

As the rut approaches, the stags may start fraying bushes and trees, and occasionally scoring the ground with their antlers. None of these fraying signs is as regular as those produced by roe, and even in woodland with high populations of reds, there may be very little evidence of bark stripping. The adult males love to wallow in wet mud or peat at this time, often urinating over their bellies and in the mud bath to help produce a rank smell. I can only assume it is attractive to the females or acts as a deterrent to other males. A wallow which has been used by deer is often quite large, at least 2 or 3 metres across, has many lines scored along the edges, from both hooves and antlers, and above all else, it smells. This scent is very, very musky. It really can be quite a thick, heady aroma, much stronger than most other animal scents. The only species likely to cause confusion is the sika deer, which displays the same wallowing habits, though the wallows of these are normally smaller, and the scent is, I think, a little sweeter.

Where deer have been browsing, they often form a distinct browse line on the vegetation, and red deer create the highest of these. Such a line is particularly noticeable in deciduous woodland, where the lowest branches are all nibbled clean of leaves to a perfectly neat and consistent level. All deer species will sometimes stand up on their hind legs to reach the choicest feed, and this can give a male red deer a browsing height of at least 2 metres.

SENSES

Hearing and smell are, as you might expect, both highly developed in this species. In my opinion, they also have the best eyesight of any British deer, and are able to spot a careless human over a kilometre away. Once again, they respond more to movement than form, though are adept at picking out even inanimate objects if these noticeably disrupt the line of the horizon. They also respond to the atmosphere which surrounds them, and a grouse taking flight may well frighten the group of deer you are trying to approach. In the same manner as roe, they are quite canny when it comes to catching you off guard, and if they suspect danger, will often put their heads down as though grazing whilst in fact they are concentrating hard on every sound, sight and scent.

SOUND ADVICE

Anyone who has been to the Scottish highlands in the early autumn and has heard the roaring of the deer must come away with a lasting memory of one of nature's most thrilling and evocative sounds. I have heard the call described variously as boving, belling, roaring and groaning, and I am sure there are many more local descriptions of this glorious declaration. It is produced by the male deer throughout the rut, and the first hint of it on a cold, still night is the most thrilling herald of the exciting time to come. The earliest I have heard it is around the middle of September, and the latest at the end of October.

It is quite unlike any other natural sound, but can best be compared with the lowing of a Hereford bull that has caught the scent of cows. Starting with this as a basis, now add strangled moans, and a sort of resonance as though the call were being produced down the inside of a hollow log. Each call may last for four or five seconds, much longer than any domestic bull, and is frequently finished off with a series of coughs or grunts, especially if the stag has been running to herd up the females. Such roars may carry over a huge distance, and if channelled by a valley or other natural theatre, can be heard at least 1.7 kilometres away.

A sound produced by all male deer is the clash of antlers during a fight, and in the red deer, this can be very loud indeed. It is the unmistakable rattle of bone on bone, often well spaced with sudden flurries of crashing and clunking. At a distance, it sounds a little like rocks being broken in a crusher.

The hinds produce a clipped, higher-pitched version of the same quality of noise, often when trying to locate a calf. This rarely lasts longer than a second, and does not carry anything like the distance of the male's rutting cries. Calves also produce a reedy version along the same lines as their mother's theme.

Moving through cover at speed, this species sounds as heavy as it is, and disturbing a herd of deer at close range can be startling for both parties. Travelling slowly through the undergrowth, however, they can be extraordinarily quiet, and there have been many occasions when a

group of red deer have walked to within 15 metres of my hiding place
before I have sensed their presence. I have never seen red deer stott.

OBSERVATION

I have used two main methods for watch-
ing and filming red deer, either using the car as a mobile hide or else
stalking on foot. Each method is suited to a different habitat. Where the
deer are using open farmland or moorland, such as on Exmoor, I have
always found the car method to be ideal. Often there are small country
lanes that wind their way through the heart of deer country, and with
the landowner's permission it may even be possible to drive into favoured
areas with a good four-wheel drive vehicle. Most of the deer I have
encountered in this way have shown very little fear of the car, and
assuming you are careful to keep downwind of the animals, it is sometimes possible to have them approach to within a few metres.

There are certain precautions you should take if using the vehicle as
a hide. It often pays to have someone else drive whilst you spot from
the passenger seat. Let land owners know that you are in the area; a lot
of poaching goes on from cars and you may find your animal watching
disrupted by having to make awkward explanations. If you are driving
on single track roads, be very careful where you decide to stop, always
use lay-byes or gateways to allow other traffic through. I often use
netting or scrim across the passenger side window if I expect to be close
to the animals, with a small observation hole cut in it at eye level.

Having found a regular feeding, resting or rutting area, it usually pays
to get there before first light, switch off the engine and wait. One of
the beauties of using the car as a hide is that if you hear or see activity
elsewhere, it is sometimes possible to get closer to it without disturbance.
If you intend to move, and can see the deer, try to pick a moment when
they are active before you start the engine. Do not move the car
immediately, but wait until any eyes or ears that are trained on you have
relaxed and gone back about their business. Do not drive in a straight
line towards the animals, but, instead, start by driving away or parallel
to them, then circle slowly around to bring your vehicle closer alongside.

If at any point the deer start to move away, do not try and keep up, they will only feel they are being chased, and will disappear altogether.

Whether using the car as a hide or stalking on foot, it can be quite difficult to pick out the form of a red deer at a distance, more so if it is in rough moorland where its colours blend well with the surrounding hues. Look out for their pale rumps; with stags, the antlers can catch the eye over quite a distance. Once you have spotted a deer, a closer inspection through binoculars will often reveal several others in the area that were invisible to the naked eye. On fields of green pasture, the red-brown of the coat can show up over quite some distance, but given that the deer often lie up close to a field border or hedgerow, even here they may be well camouflaged.

If you intend to stalk this species on foot, remain constantly aware of your outline against the horizon. In open moorland or hill country this may well mean crawling on your belly for some distance. If you find yourself having to do this, remember you have got a bottom. I have seen many people crawling along with their head nicely close to the ground, but with their behinds sticking up and waving around like a beacon to the deer. In a crawl, the highest point should be your eyes and these should only just be above the level of the vegetation. Stop all your movement if any one of the deer you are trying to approach looks up.

The rut is one of the most exciting times to watch reds, and possibly one of the easiest from the point of view of locating them. This, of course, is by virtue of the stags' phenomenal calls which carry over such huge distances. Though the deer do visit traditional areas for the rut, the stags may not remain sedentary in their stands (a small area defended against all other males). In some habitats, one adult may well occupy an area of a hectare or more, and is likely to leave this area if he detects nearby wandering females. One of the limiting factors which affects the size of a stand and how faithfully the stag sticks to it, may be the number of active males in the area. In places where the density is high, I have noticed the largest, most active stags keeping to fairly small areas, chasing and herding the hind within invisible boundaries, but not pursuing beyond. Should an adult male test these boundaries and cross into the stand of an adjacent stag who is equally matched a fight may ensue. These tests of strength and dominance are surely one of the greatest natural spectacles the British Isles have to offer.

Though I have watched many fights, I have always found the conditions under which they occurred to vary substantially. The best opportunity of witnessing such an act is along the border of a rutting stand, but to predict precisely where is very tricky. Sometimes, by listening to the calls made by the stags you can pin-point a likely opponent and position yourself in such a way that you are between the two well matched males. Once a fight has started it is sometimes possible to get very close to the action, so preoccupied are the combatants.

PHOTOGRAPHY

It is well worth considering how you are going to keep your camera stable if you plan to use a car as a hide or stalk in open country. I have found that the best mount for a stills camera with a long lens used in a car is a bean-bag. This can be draped over the door with the window wound down and offers snug support for even the most unwieldy lenses. A refined version of this incorporates the attachment of a small platform on to the door, with adjustable height, providing a more comfortable and stable plinth for the bean-bag to rest on. It is possible to use a bean-bag when stalking, though much of the deer country is covered with heather which is too tall for a clear shot from the ground. A standard tripod is often too tall for this purpose, forcing you to stick your head and gear up above the line of the horizon. There are small tripods which are ideal for this application, and with a ball and socket head attached, provide a quick, wobble-free and unobtrusive support system.

Fallow Deer

(Dama dama)

Of all the deer species found in the British Isles, this is the one I have watched and filmed most extensively. They are one of the most ubiquitous deer species, and one of the most approachable, particularly in parks and estates where herds are kept to grace the landscape. They are probably the most variable species of deer to look at, with colour ranging from black through all shades of brown, to white. But whatever their colour or setting, they are always a joy to watch.

WHERE AND WHEN

Fallow occur all over the British mainland, either in parks and collections, farms, or in the truly wild state. The stronghold for the wild deer is in the south and south east of England, with good populations in the New Forest, Hampshire, the forests of Dorset, and woodlands surrounding Sussex and Surrey. There are many other smaller pockets of fallow deer in southern rural England, plus a few in south Wales, the Midlands and Scotland. Despite being a species introduced to the British Isles, they are nonetheless very much part of rural Britain, and seem as much a part of the temperate woodlands they frequent as any badger or fox.

The range of opportunities that exist for watching this lovely creature is enormous. In all situations, the fallow deer are animals of woodland and open parkland. They show a distinct preference for open glades surrounded by thick cover, though in the New Forest often frequent the lowland heaths. They tend to prefer grazing to browsing, though this differs according to the time of year and available food supply.

Their year is well structured and predictable, and is quite different for the bucks and the does. The females form distinct herds with the fawns and sometimes first year bucks or prickets. Young are born in late May and June. Like other deer, the does tend to move away, or perhaps more accurately, fall behind the main herd when they are about to give birth. A doe nearing labour starts to walk in tight circles, often sniffing or licking her vulva, and repeatedly lies down in a restless manner. Within a few hours of birth, the young deer is able to walk and competently follow its mother, even if she breaks into a run. The fawns tire quickly and will often curl up in thick cover, particularly if their dam senses danger, and remain motionless until retrieved to suckle. After about a week, the fawns are following their mother much more of the time, and will begin to socialize with the other newborn members of the doe herd.

During the long summer evenings, the fawns play games of chase, 'king of the castle', and a crazy form of 'follow-my-leader', sometimes joined by their mothers. The end of June through July are the best times for watching this sort of behaviour. As the summer comes to an end, the doe herds tend to split up into smaller groups as the time of rut approaches. In early autumn the does move to the traditional rutting stands, and one by one are mated with by the fittest and strongest buck of the day. Many of the best rutting stands are in areas of rich feeding, and the does often seem very casual about the whole affair, wandering into the arena nibbling acorns, mating, and wandering out again. During this time, the growing fawns seem fairly bemused, even a little nervous of the activities of the aggressive bucks, and though a few precocious female fawns may mate in their first year, most do not until their second.

Immediately after they have mated the female deer move away from the rutting stands to feed well on the autumnal bounty of nuts and fruits. All fallow deer are particularly fond of chestnuts, both horse and sweet, and where these trees exist in fallow deer country, you will be certain to find the animals. They are also very partial to apples and may well raid orchards as the fruit ripens. As their dark winter coat starts to develop in late autumn, the does will be discouraging their offspring from suckling if they have not already done so, though I have seen does nursing their young well into December. Winter is spent with the females in small groups accompanied by their well grown young, the males of which will be growing their first set of antlers, visible as single furry spikes. The company of these young males is gradually shunned by their mothers, and as their antlers harden and clean in the spring, they are given short shrift and forced to leave their natal company to form gangs of adolescent bucks, often joining up with two and three-year-old animals.

The buck herds remain distinct, and to a great extent, faithful to an age bracket. Normally, the prickets (first year bucks with single antler spikes) and sorrels (second year animals with more recognizable tined and palmated antlers) form frisky, inquisitive gangs: the more mature bucks, of three to five years of age, tend to stick together. The true master bucks—huge creatures with magnificent antlers—often keep themselves to themselves, and may form groups of eight or ten, many of which have the same members from one year to the next.

The buck's year starts with the loss of its old antlers, which are cast during the end of March through April. The older bucks lose their antlers earlier than the younger ones, and this may help to explain why the male deer form herds of a similar age. In fallow deer society most disputes between males are sorted out with the antlers, and a dominance hierarchy often relates directly to the age, strength, and general grandeur of the bucks. I once saw a mature buck which had recently lost his antlers, savagely attacked by a younger male, a scenario that would occur frequently if the bucks remained in mixed age herds.

With the antlers lost, the bucks settle down to some serious feeding, grazing on lush summer herbs and grasses, and browsing on fresh green leaves. They often stick to a regular timetable during this season, lying up during the middle part of the day to rest and digest, coming out in the evening to feed, often in open glades and rides. Like red deer, in summer the fallow bucks sport fat bellies and skinny necks, hardly the picture of majestic strength many people suppose them to be. The antlers grow throughout the period, until August and September, when the velvet dries and is frayed off. The bucks are vigorous in their attempts to rid themselves of the protective skin, thrashing bushes and scraping trees in the process, and it is now that antagonistic behaviour starts amongst the herd.

It is usually the youngest animals that start the sparring matches that later may develop into full-blown fights, the more mature animals saving their strength for the rut proper. By mid-September, the breeding males are starting to come into condition, and have splintered into smaller groups or individual animals as they make their way to the traditional rutting stands. A mature buck in rutting condition is one of the most awesome sights of wild Britain. His waist has narrowed and strengthened, and his great, broad antlers have been burnished to a bronzed polish by repeated rubbing against tree-trunks. The once skinny neck is now enormously thick and muscular and reveals a pronounced lump on the underside, a developed Adam's apple ready for proclamation of intent. His chest and rump also reveal remarkable muscle definition, and his coat is starting to adopt the darker tones of winter. (Some deer are always pale, either a ginger colour known as menil or completely white.)

Fallow are probably the species of deer most faithful to a rutting ground. Year after year, certain stands of trees, or even individual clearings, are used by the most dominant bucks to attract as many mates as possible, and are defended vehemently against all others. Even in open parkland, with little or no visual boundaries to the stands, the bucks rarely defend an area much more than 50 or 60 metres across. The most dramatic of all rutting areas that I have ever watched is in the New Forest, where certain oak plantations have been the setting for the bucks' titanic battles year after year. These glades of mature trees, criss-crossed by boundary ditches, offer the field naturalist ideal cover and clear views of the central activity. The first grunts from the bucks are usually heard in late September, but it is not until mid-October that the rut gets truly under way. If picking a single date to watch the fallow rut, it would be 21 October, for some reason a time which has always provided the most frenetic activity wherever I have been observing the behaviour. If the morning has been frosty and the skies clear around this time, you are in for a real treat of courtship, fighting and breeding displays. The rut continues to the end of October, but peters out quickly afterwards, when the exhausted bucks begin to regroup to form winter herds.

Whilst looking for a good location for watching the deer, try to concentrate on areas where the ground is flat or sweeps away from you in a basin, with sparse but consistent cover. Stretches of ground which are densely forested or where hilly country shortens the view are frustrating for the naturalist.

TRACK AND SIGN

Fallow leave many of the same clues to their whereabouts as the other species of deer. Their paths or runs are only marginally wider than those created by roe deer, but the tracks left on soft ground are noticeably longer, broader and more rounded. A mature buck will leave quite deep slots on damp soil, and where their range overlaps with that of the red deer, this may be confused with the red's even more solidly built sign. Fallow tend to meander through woodland and pasture in a more arbitrary way than roe, and so are less likely to leave such well defined runs.

The droppings are similar in shape to those of other deer, and as you might expect, are intermediate in size between those of the roe and red. Fallow share the roe deer's habit of lying up in a cleared area, and such lies are often marked by clusters of dung. The shape of each dropping has a marginally more pronounced nipple at one end and depression at the other than those of other deer. Their colour is usually black to dark brown. Fallow are not prone to indulge in a great deal of fraying apart for a brief period during and just after the time when the velvet is lost. Patches on branches and narrow tree trunks, which look more as though they have been polished than scraped, are often the work of the bucks, and such marks are usually at a height of a metre or so above the ground. Fallow sometimes scrape the ground with their fore feet, particularly on the lead up to and during the rut, either as a prelude to lying down, or sometimes whilst worrying at a bush with their antlers. These scrapes are fairly randomly formed and rarely as well defined a fan shape as those made by roe deer.

Where the deer have been feeding on chestnuts, particularly conkers, a litter of opened husks is evident beneath the tree. Unlike husks which have split naturally, one which has been mouthed by a fallow usually bears cracks and splits across the casing, and if fresh, will be covered in saliva. Indeed, it is quite remarkable watching these creatures deal with the spiky shells, rolling them around their mouths, and allowing the waste to fall to the ground.

Fallow fur is very variable in colour, but nonetheless quite distinctive. The winter coat is usually dark brown on the tip, pale at the base, coarse and with very slight corrugations. It is not as long or as thick as red deer fur and lacks the dark reddish tint. The summer coat varies from white to sandy brown and black, but all are fairly short (2–3 cm) thick and never as red as that of a roe or red deer. There is a good chance of confusion with sika, but fallow hair is usually shorter and paler.

Like other deer, fallow do not leave a scent we can detect at any time other than during the rut. In the early autumn, the bucks produce a thick, heady musk, which, if you are downwind, is powerful enough to carry several hundred metres. I have found rutting stands by their scent alone. It is particularly strong in the areas of bare soil scraped by the bucks on their stands, and where they frequently urinate.

SOUND ADVICE

There are four main calls produced by fallow: an alarm bark; a contact call, one by the doe, another by the fawns; and the rutting calls of the bucks.

The alarm bark can be heard at any time of year and is a sign that an unidentified danger has been spotted. It does not mean that your cover has been blown, and surrounding deer take surprisingly little notice of one of their rank who is barking. It is similar to the alarm bark of a roe deer, but less harsh, and not as low in pitch. Its more open tone may be described as 'Bah', and it is usually uttered singly and well spaced. Like the alarm bark of the roe, it can be pretty startling if heard at close quarters in a woodland at dusk.

The doe's contact call, usually made when searching for a lost fawn, is a medium-pitched, almost crow-like 'Maa', produced frequently until the stray has been located. Each call lasts no more than half a second and descends in pitch towards the end. The call of a fawn, is a variation on the same theme, but is much higher-pitched and suggests more of a sound resembling, 'maow.' It has a very nasal, reedy quality, and I have only heard it uttered when the youngster is lost or answering its dam.

Bucks will sometimes produce a call similar to that of the doe, but it is always much quieter, and associated more with the younger bucks. I have never heard a mature buck make any sound during the summer other than an alarm bark.

With the approach of the rut, the male deer find their voice. Fallow buck calls are described variously as grunting, belching or bellowing. Personally, I think the middle term is most apt, because a buck proclaiming his strength and intentions sounds for all the world like a huge beast with a terrible dose of indigestion. The belching calls can carry over a great distance and are produced at a rate of roughly one a second. A buck can keep up this vocal display for hours on end, particularly if any does or rival bucks are present, but calls are normally given in bouts of eight or nine grunts, followed by a rest of a few seconds and so on. The only change in pitch or length of the call that I have noticed occurs when the buck covers the doe, when he produces a single, long, drawn out belch which may last two to three seconds. Each buck has quite a distinctive voice and it is often possible to discern several individuals in a wooded area by their calls alone.

Fallow tread very quietly through woodland and may well appear close by with little or no warning. Sounds of feeding, fighting and running are similar to those of other deer. If frightened they will stott, the stiff-legged prancing gait which results in most neighbouring deer becoming alert and wary. This action makes a distinctive thumping sound, often added to by crashing vegetation. The spacing of the thumps depends on the speed and size of the deer, but five or six in a row, starting with two a second and ending rather faster gives an average guide.

OBSERVATION

Fallow can be treated in much the same manner as red deer, and most filming that I have done of this species has been either from a vehicle or by staking out likely locations. When settling on a place to wait and watch for the deer, pay special attention to background cover, as they are particularly adept at picking out a human form, even when it is completely stationary. As with other deer, good camouflage is essential, especially around the head and shoulder area.

If you are keen on watching the rutting behaviour, then finding the right spot is everything. Some of the most active stands can be in quite thick forest and though the sounds are magnificent at such locations, reverberating from tree to tree, the views can sometimes be frustratingly obscured. In park and estate herds, the view is often unobstructed, but the spirit of the event is somewhat dissipated by such wide open spaces.

The most thrilling rutting behaviour I have ever watched took place amongst a tall stand of oaks, beneath which the forest floor was open and fairly clear of bushes and shrubs. I was positioned in a ditch running along the downwind edge of a clearing which was well trampled and had all the signs of being the centre of activity. Before settling on this site, I had looked at several others, and made a careful point of listening to the bucks' calls to try and pin-point their positions in each. The first time I visited what was to be the chosen site, with the guidance of a forest keeper, I managed to crawl up to the edge of the stand whilst the buck was attempting to round up a group of females, and was able to confirm that all the elements for a potentially great view were there.

The next morning, having made myself as comfortable as possible, with only my head and camera (both covered in camouflage netting) poking above ground level, I awaited the first confirmation that my approach had been sufficiently subtle. After about twenty minutes, the grunts from a rutting deer, which must have been at least 500 or 600 metres away, rang between the great wooden pillars of the forest. Then a startlingly loud belch came from somewhere to my right. In the half light I strained to catch the form of the buck and could vaguely make out his stocky frame walking over the ditch some 10 metres away and out into the clearing ahead of me.

The following eight or nine hours provided me with some of the most thrilling moments I have ever been privileged to witness in wild Britain. At one point in the late afternoon, with saffron light streaming through the oaks, two of the biggest bucks engaged in the mightiest combat. Their complete preoccupation with the battle brought them to within a metre of my hiding place, completely oblivious of my presence.

When using the car as a mobile hide, the deer are invariably aware of your presence and only accept you if their experiences of human beings in vehicles have all been benign. It is still possible to get some cracking good views, however, and this is often the best method of observing the deer if you are trying to track a more mobile aspect of the animals' behaviour, such as antler casting.

All of the rules which apply to watching red deer from a vehicle also apply to this species, and I have found most fallow to be extremely accommodating when watched in this way.

PHOTOGRAPHY

I have found fallow to be one of the easiest deer to photograph and record on film and the first shot I ever took on a professional cine camera was indeed of this species. Park deer offer ideal opportunities to hone your photographic and film-making skills, and though some may border on completely tame, there will be enough in a herd which regard you with suspicion to make achieving a good sequence or photograph something of which to be proud.

Sika Deer

(Cervus nippon)

My experience with this species is limited, because I have only watched them in the south of England and primarily during the rut.

WHERE AND WHEN

Originally from Japan, sika have now spread to many parts of mainland UK, and some of the smaller islands in the south. They are quite prolific in the forests of southern Dorset, in certain enclosures of the New Forest in Hampshire, and a population thrives on Brownsea island in Poole Harbour, having apparently swum across from the mainland. The only other large population that I am aware of is around Inverness and the Mull of Kintyre, Scotland, where the forests bordering some of the lochs play host to good numbers. Smaller pockets of this species crop up from time to time in widely spaced regions, most of which can be attributed to escapees from deer farms and private collections.

This is a real forest deer, browsing on everything from hazel buds to conifers and only occasionally coming out to graze on herbs and grasses. They are typically found in mixed woodland with alternate dense cover and open rides and glades, often skulking around the edges of the clearings keeping an eye out for danger, and this, too, is the sort of habitat most conducive to observing them.

Their year follows much the same pattern as that of the red deer, but with most events taking place one or two weeks earlier. They also have one of the most extended rutting periods of any species of deer found in Europe, the first calls being heard around the first or second week of September, and continuing right up to December on occasions. The peak of rutting activity is usually around the third or last week of September, with many of the most ferocious fights being settled a week before this. Sika are to my eyes one of the most aggressive deer, and a battle between two well matched stags can be frighteningly fierce, often resulting in broken antlers and sometimes injury to one or both parties. The rutting stands are far less sedentary than those made by fallow deer, and though a dominant stag may trot around a small patch of woodland chasing the female deer for an hour or so, he is also just as likely to wander off in search of new and interesting relationships. This trait can make watching this species quite tricky, but hot-spots of activity do sometimes persist for several days, giving the field naturalist a chance for some extended viewing.

TRACK AND SIGN

Signs that are uniquely sika are few and far between. The footprint is typical of all deer, and somewhere in size between that of a roe and a fallow. Hair varies from a ginger-brown colour in summer to a dark brown, almost black, in autumn and winter. The most noticeable characteristic of sika fur is its length, often much longer than that of any other British deer species, apart from red deer, giving the animal a positively shaggy look in the field. I have only found sika hair on a few occasions, and each time it has kept me guessing for a moment or two. The dark winter coat is the most frequently encountered, bearing very slight corrugations and a pale tip.

One of the most distinctive sika signs is the wallow. The only other British species which indulges in the same sort of behaviour is the red, which by comparison often makes larger scrapes in much more open country. A sika stag in full rut will scrape an area of moist ground with his feet and antlers and roll into the slushy pit. After a short while these wallows reek of musk and can be located by their scent alone in dense woodland. The largest I have seen was about 2 metres across, roughly circular, and very smelly.

The stags also score the ground and trees with their antlers, leaving straight gouges which are unlike any roe fraying-marks or fallow burnishing-patches. The stags may also have mock fights with grass tussocks, leaving whole clumps uprooted.

As you scour the countryside for signs of wild creatures, bear in mind that domestic animals may leave confusing tracks and clumps of hair on wire fences. When finding hair you do not recognise, first look to see what, if any, animal is living in the field beyond. Probably the greatest confusion comes from certain goats, some of which have hair uncannily like a deer's, and from dogs, which come in all thicknesses and hues. Dog hair is difficult to rule out completely, simply because of its diverse range, but nonetheless there are a couple of pointers which should help. First and most importantly is the thickness and feel. The creature most likely to be confused with dog is fox, whose hair is considerably finer, lighter, softer and usually straighter than any of its domestic cousins, and it is this relatively thick and wiry feel which sets dogs apart. The second indicator that you have found dog hair is the colour, which though approximating some deer, fox or other wild animal's pelage, never bears all of the same characteristics of shape, length and width. Goat hair is normally all one colour along its length, unlike most deer's which have subtle grades of colour from base to tip.

SOUND ADVICE

Like most deer, sika stags only find their full vocal range during the rut, and it's extensive. The blood-curdling groans of this creature sound at the very least as if someone nearby was being tortured to death. The rutting scream starts with a high, harmonic whistle, which slowly descends in pitch until it reaches a quality and tone not unlike a person in great pain. At this point the whistle turns into a mournful groan, quite human in quality, which wavers and peters out as in the manner of a final, gasping breath. This call is often made even more eerie by the stag's throaty laugh, a sound often produced as the animal trots after another stag, chasing it out of the stand. It resembles a deep, demonic chuckle, and combined with the scream, produces a very unnerving chorus.

A third call associated with the rut is the tri-whistle. This incorporates the same pitch and quality as the start of the whistle-groan, but is more abrupt and ends before any voice-like quality is produced. As the name of the call suggests, it is normally uttered in batches of three, though this can vary among individuals. All of these whistles are very hard to reproduce with the human mouth, due to their harmonic qualities. The most familiar sound I know which approximates their pitch is that produced by a child's toy. This corrugated length of plastic pipe is held at one end, and rapidly spun in a circle over the head, producing an airy, discordant whistle which varies in pitch depending on the speed it is travelling. The sound this toy makes is so like a whistling sika, that I considered taking one with me into the field to see what effect my mimicry would have on the locals.

The alarm snort is a nasal explosion that sounds a bit like someone trying to spit a fly off the end of their tongue. This call is often heard in a sort of rally, as first one, then three or four other deer produce it in quick succession. When uncertain of an object this species may stott, stiff-legged, with their white rump hair fanned out wide if they suspect danger. As with other species of deer, these displays often mean that the deer are unsettled but have not yet confirmed the identity or position of a potential threat, so if you hear these sounds, remain motionless and silent, and you may well find they settle again surprisingly quickly. Hind and calves produce a high-pitched bleating when communicating.

OBSERVATION

Almost all of my sika observation has been achieved using a vehicle as a hide, though I have also stalked through woodland to reach active rutting stands. The greatest problem

I have found with the latter method is trying to remain silent whilst moving through the heavily forested habitat which the deer tend to frequent. Often I would see the deer, but unless they were using a cleared area, the views would be brief and I was constantly running the risk of disturbing an animal before ever catching a glimpse of it.

By driving around forest tracks, or along the edges of well used clearings in a four-wheel drive vehicle, I have managed to get many clear and close views of this species. The mature stags are typically more nervous than many of the younger animals and females, but even they are frequently relaxed about the close proximity of a vehicle.

PHOTOGRAPHY

Use the same techniques as for red deer.

Muntjac

(Muntiacus reevesi)

The last, and in some ways the least, of the deer species I will deal with. Least because of their diminutive size and the minimal observation I have made of them.

WHERE AND WHEN

This tiny deer is locally common in the south and south east of England, in wooded areas and parkland or garden habitats. In some parts it has become an unwelcome visitor to ornamental gardens, where it exhibits a passion for browsing on various flowers and shrubs, a habit which goes down like a cup of cold mud with keen horticulturalists! My own views of this charming little newcomer to British fauna have been restricted to a population which was released on Steep Holm, a 20-hectare island in the middle of the Bristol Channel, one or two fleeting glimpses in woodland around Surrey, a few more prolonged views in Hertfordshire gardens and captive animals.

TRACK AND SIGN

Whichever habitat they frequent, they are tricky creatures to spot by virtue of their size—about that of a small to medium-sized dog. They move quietly and hesitantly through their territories, and in thick cover are extremely easy to overlook. During my two month stay on Steep Holm, filming the gull colony which nests there, I only saw muntjac on about five occasions. Most of these were fleeting glimpses of a russet back as the animal dashed through the thick ground vegetation, but a couple of sightings were more prolonged, and allowed me to have a marginally more intimate view of this elusive critter.

As you might expect, the footprints are like a tiny version of a roe deer's, and could be confused with those of a roe fawn or possibly the slightly larger Chinese water deer.

Dung, too, is tiny, about the size of a rabbit dropping, but typically deer-shaped and coloured—shiny black and oval, with a point at one end and a depression at the other. I have always found these in loose clusters, often close to an area used to lie up.

The hair is roughly the same colour as that of a roe in its summer coat, but is slightly more brown, and is not corrugated. The muntjac on Steep Holm had little or no visible effect on what little tree growth there was on the island, though having watched a tame, captive animal scraping and gouging fence posts with his antlers, I would expect there to be some fraying or tree scoring sign where populations were dense.

One of the traits I have also noticed with captive muntjac is their almost continuous use of scent glands, situated along the top of the forehead, leading down to the eye from the antler. Bucks particularly indulge in much rubbing against trees and posts with these glands, which exude an oily musk, and may stain the areas where this repeatedly happens. They also have a very large gland just below the eye, which can be inverted like a little grape, and this produces a tar-like secretion which also smells musky.

I know very little about this species' rutting behaviour, only that they are capable of breeding at any time of year and that most activity I have noted has taken place around August, the males becoming very aggressive at this time. Antlers I have seen cast have been lost around May and June, and new growth is clean of velvet by autumn.

SOUND ADVICE

The vocal sounds of this deer are unique, and closely resemble a dog's. I have only heard this sound produced by deer in the wild state and am uncertain of its meaning. It may be an alarm call, though I doubt this, because it has never been produced in response to my presence. Far more likely is that it is a contact call, produced by an animal in search of company and related to courtship. They also produce a gentle smacking noise whilst opening and closing their scent glands.

OBSERVATION AND PHOTOGRAPHY

Most of the sightings I have had of this species have been serendipitous. The only exceptions have been in suburban gardens where the animals may occasionally follow a fairly predictable routine of feeding and resting, and may well ignore all but the most sudden and noisy of human activities. Under these conditions general observation techniques that apply to other deer species are successful.

The Hedgehog

(Erinaceus europaeus)

Hedgehogs are not exactly shy, elusive, hard-to-see creatures. But they are nonetheless one of the most popular of all European wild animals, and can go unnoticed in your own back yard unless you recognize the signs which betray them. They can also provide you with fantastic views of a completely wild creature going about its business, without having to worry about camouflage or hiding, and this alone is a rare treat.

WHERE AND WHEN

Hedgehogs are now widely distributed around Europe, but, locally, can be extremely rare. Just what governs the distribution of this little insect-eater is a bit of a mystery to me. They do not like cold marshland, or motor cars.

Above: Not all wild animals move away from you. Herring gulls are very vigorous in their defence of eggs and young, and will dive repeatedly at an intruder, striking out with their feet and sometimes drawing blood from an unwary human head.

Above: By carefully watching a fox's breeding earth, you may be treated to some very intimate views, as the parents return to feed their cubs.

Left: Because of many mute swans' apparent indifference to human presence, they are ideal subjects for close and intimate observation. By watching animals like these you can concentrate on attempting to see the unusual events in their lives with little risk of disturbing them.

And where badgers are common, hedgehogs are rare. If you have ever seen a badger dealing with this prickly parcel of meat, perhaps you will understand why. Of all the predators in Britain, badgers seem best equipped to deal with hedgehogs as a meal, digging a shallow pit next to the curled pin-cushion, rolling it in with muzzle or fore feet, and then using enormous power and long front claws to prize open the packed lunch. This whole procedure is usually punctuated by very loud and pitiful screams and grunts coming from the terrified hedgehog. Given that these little animals can only curl up and hope for the best if discovered, it stands to reason that they may be infrequent or even absent in good brocky country.

The most likely place to see a hedgehog is, of course, flat in the middle of the road. The next most likely spot is in a suburban garden, and if your own patch does not have a regular visitation from a hedgehog, then someone nearby almost certainly will. The further north and higher above sea level you live, the less chance you have of encountering this lovely beast. Equally if you are surrounded by farmland which has been intensively managed with pesticides, your hedgehog population will be low, because their main food supply will have taken a hammering.

A lot of a hedgehog's year is spent in hibernation, a state of torpor adopted to see through the lean cold months of winter. This is not to say that a hedgehog will not ever rouse from this state during the winter

Left: Many small mammals are best photographed in captivity, although ensuring the welfare of the animal is of paramount importance. Most species are protected by law and can only be handled if you have been granted a special licence.

months. In fact, they have short periods of activity quite regularly, when their heart beat returns to normal and they fidget around inside the hibernation nest for an hour or so. If there is a particularly warm spell, they may even be tempted to come outside for a quick wander around. This winter activity is particularly common among young animals which did not manage to put on a substantial fat reserve before entering hibernation, and which are likely to starve if they don't try to find a meal during a warm winter spell. Sadly, slugs, beetles and worms are few and far between at this time and a skinny young animal seen wandering about is unlikely to make it through to the spring.

The first hedgehogs normally emerge in March, and year after year I have judged the start of spring based on the first squashed hog I have seen on the road. Their main objective is to find a good meal, in the form of any invertebrates (insects, etc) they come across. Their next objective is to find a mate, and April and May is the first period of the year that hedgehogs are likely to be seen indulging in courtship. Young are usually born in June in a specially created nursery den, and are totally dependent on their mother for the first few weeks of their life. These nursery nests sometimes turn up in the most unlikely places, from cardboard boxes stored in the garden shed, to one I saw in a blanket, tossed into the corner of a concrete and regularly used garage. Mid to late July is when most hedgehog families start to wander around together, and there are few sights more charming than a large mother hog, followed by four or five spiky replicas, snuffling in a line across the lawn.

Another period during which courtship and mating may occur takes place during mid- to late summer, and the offspring born as a result often arrive too late to survive the winter in hibernation. The only chance such tiny animals have of making it through is if helped by someone who is prepared to take them into care until spring, keeping them warm and feeding them, to be released when the warmer weather arrives.

TRACK AND SIGN

There are two regular hedgehog signs: their

droppings and their nests. The latter can be quite hard to find, but dung is left liberally and randomly as the animal feeds. Typically, it shows up on lawns or in vegetable plots, a smallish, inky-black, squiggly sort of dropping, which, on close inspection, often reveals bits of beetle casing and other bug fragments within. The colour can be variable, particularly if the hedgehog has been bingeing on worms and slugs, which produce a greenish-brown deposit. Regardless of colour, the size (roughly 4 to 6 cm long and 1-1.5 cm wide) and shape will identify it; I have never noticed any characteristic smell to them. It is not uncommon to find four or five droppings on a lawn after a single night's feeding.

Hedgehog nests, both summer and winter, are usually built amongst a tangle of branches, such as the heart of a bramble bush, or at the base of a large coppiced shrub, and are always at or about ground level. The entrance to the summer nest is often plugged with vegetation, and is also well camouflaged. There is very little sign that it is used, except, perhaps, for a slightly trampled pathway leading up to the last metre or so before the entrance. Summer nests may be built under sheds, in the corners of outhouses, in log piles, or virtually anywhere to which the hogs can get easy, ground level access, and which remains dry. A hibernating hedgehog will often build its nest within some protective structure, such as a log pile, the base of a hollow tree, or between the crevices of a stone wall.

The nests themselves vary from little more than a bundle of dry leaves to a fairly elaborate dome of sticks, grasses and dry vegetation. A classic, and rather misguided, site for a nest is in the heart of a pile of garden refuse, the sticks, leaves, and soil providing an ideal retreat. Before ever burning a heap of garden rubbish it is wise to turn the whole lot over gently, preferably with gloved hands instead of the garden fork, just to be sure that your garden pest control unit has not set up residence inside.

Hedgehog footprints are distinctive, but rare. In a year and a half of making a film on this species, the only time I saw a print was when working on a sequence next to a bit of marshland, where wet mud and a very tame hog produced some lovely examples. They looked rather like the track left by a brown rat, though lacked any of the lines which rats often leave by dragging their tails. The clearest I saw revealed four little forward-pointing toes, each with a tiny but clearly defined claw mark, and despite the hedgehog's apparent width, they formed a surprisingly straight line, with only a small offset for left and right feet. The pads of the feet were well marked on some, completely absent on others, and this reflects the tip-toe gait the animal often adopts.

Where a hedgehog has been feeding, there is usually nothing of the meal left to betray this. The only exception I know is where the meal has been predominantly of slugs, which though enjoyed by the hogs, are apparently somewhat difficult to deal with. The result can be little lumps of congealed slug slime, often including a bit of the gut, wiped off the mouth on to the lawn or soil of the vegetable patch. Caterpillars, beetles, worms, etc, are all munched in their entirety.

SENSES

Most hedgehogs do not regard human beings as much of a threat. They will freeze if they hear something they do not recognize as safe, and their hearing is pretty good. Their sense of smell is also highly developed, but I have never noticed a negative response from an animal which was downwind of me.

SOUND ADVICE

For such a little critter, hedgehogs produce some extraordinarily big noises. The sound most commonly produced is snuffling, half way between a puff of wind and a grunt. It is often made if the hog feels a bit threatened, and I associate it with the animal bringing its forward spines down over its face in defence. It is also produced when two hogs come together, particularly if a push and shove battle develops between them. Such encounters are quite common, and some may be a prelude to mating. Courtship is a generally noisy affair, with much puffing, grunting and wheezing from both parties.

Hedgehogs are capable of producing a remarkable scream of alarm, which sounds very like a squealing pig, and may well have something to do with the derivation of their name. They used to feature on the menu of many a countryman in Britain, apparently coated in clay and baked alive. They most certainly would have had every good reason to squeal.

Baby hogs make a high-pitched tweeting sound, very like a bird, either if disturbed, or if hungry and missing their mother's milk. It is a very pure, almost trilling note, produced in rapid short bursts by one or more of the litter at the same time. I have never heard this sound in the wild, only from young animals bred in captivity, and though piercing, its volume is such that you would have to be very close to a nest in the field to hear it clearly. Once the young are mobile and following their mother, they produce sounds similar to those of the adults.

Of the mechanical sounds created by hedgehogs, both movement and feeding can be useful indicators of their whereabouts. A hog walking across the lawn makes very little sound, but the same creature pushing through the base of a bush or through dead leaves creates a veritable cacophony. The action of spines against dry vegetation of any kind is a distinctive give-away of a hedgehog's location. They are also very noisy eaters, never more so than when munching beetles and snails, whose hard outer casing produces a mouth-watering crunchy sound, like somebody eating a bag of potato crisps, with the occasional mushy bit.

OBSERVATION

Watching hedgehogs in the wild is surprisingly challenging. Indeed, simply finding one when you want to is no mean feat. Most hogs are completely nocturnal; an animal which is abroad by day usually has something wrong with it. One of the most active periods is about half an hour or so after sunset, and this is a good time to start your search. Use your ears at least as much as your eyes. If there is no moon and you must use a torch, try to find one which is dim or put a coloured filter across the lens to subdue the beam. Keep your own movements quiet, especially your footsteps, because hedgehogs freeze when they hear a foreign sound and, even if close by, can be remarkably tricky to discern amongst the undergrowth if they are not moving. Having found your local hog, keep a comfortable distance, about 3 to 5 metres is usually sufficient. Some hogs are much more nervous than others, and if you find that the one you are following keeps its spines partially erect, or continually stops and adopts a defensive position, either increase your following distance, or give up and find another subject. It is well known that hedgehogs will come to food which is proffered, providing you with beautifully clear and extended views. Unfortunately, the traditional hedgehog meal of bread and milk is not good for them. This is rather a pity, because they seem to relish the flavour and become hooked on their daily visits to the milk bar, but the effect of the milk on their digestive system is at best unnatural and at worst potentially fatal, because it can cause severe diarrhoea. Far better to provide some sort of meat-based feed, such as tinned dog food, or, if you are really enthusiastic, try digging up a few worms, or scouring your cabbages for caterpillars: these will be devoured with alacrity.

Though I would not recommend handling a wild hedgehog too frequently, it does little or no harm to pick one up for a short while if you want to check its sex and generally get a closer look. Though it is relatively easy to get a grip on these prickly parcels using gloved hands, all that you will see is a ball of spines. The most successful way of lifting a hedgehog without damaging either party involves a fairly delicate balance between treating it like fine porcelain and juggling. Presented with a stationary, partially curled hog, gently slip the inside of one hand, palm facing upwards, under the front end of the animal. You will feel some spines but should also be able to detect the softer fur and warmth of the underbelly. Now slip your other hand gently under the hog's rear in the same manner and slowly lift. At this point the hedgehog may well have a go at rolling up completely, so to counter this, slowly and gently rock your hands up and down a little, in a sort of rolling, see-saw action and the hog should begin to uncurl and place its feet on your hands, front pair on one, back feet on the other. Now you can carefully hold the animal's back against your chest, keeping its head uppermost. Male hogs have a large space between their anus and penis; females have only a short stretch of furry skin between their urethra and anus. This technique takes a bit of practise to perfect, but the trick is always to move slowly, gently and quietly. Having taken a good look, replace the hog precisely where you found it as soon as possible, stand away at a distance, and ensure that it walks off as happily as when first discovered.

Hedgehogs do carry fleas, and, yes, they are very obvious, simply because the widely spaced spines reveal a great deal more than the hair of most other mammals. No, they do not leap straight on to a human at the first opportunity, and if you do get one on you, it will leave very quickly because it is host specific.

PHOTOGRAPHY

Hedgehogs are tricky to keep up with in the truly wild state, and even trickier to photograph unless food has been put out for them. It is possible to use a sort of flash/torch/camera rig (see the section on photographing badgers at night), but this will only afford a record of the animals, rarely anything more dramatic. To make a film about hedgehogs, I sought permission from what was then the Nature Conservancy Council, and is now English Nature, to keep a number of animals in enclosures for just over a year. They thrived under these conditions, but they demanded a great deal of constant attention, with daily cleaning, feeding, watering, bedding changes, etc, etc. They do not make good pets. If you intend to work with one in captivity, first ensure you have sought the necessary permissions to do so, and then only keep the animal for as short a period as possible.

Most hedgehogs respond quite indifferently to flash photography and learn to accept constant artificial light after a very short period. Much of the filming I have done with them has involved the construction of artificial sets: sections of habitat recreated in a studio using natural vegetation, rocks and logs. Because the hogs are quite slow-moving, no barrier is required around the set, though it often pays to have someone else nearby to herd the hogs when they wander off the edge. It is very important that you only work with each animal for a short period, half an hour at most, and much less if it continues to try and move away from the area. A sprinkle of dog food smeared here and there around the set does wonders to convince any reluctant star that acting can be great fun.

The Shrews

(Soricidae)

There are three species of shrew common in the UK: the pygmy, the water shrew, and most common of all, the common shrew. All are protected by law, and with good reason: they are incredibly highly strung animals which require enormous amounts of food.

Common and Pygmy Shrews

(Sorex araneus, Sorex minutus)

These tiny insect-eaters (the pygmy shrew is the smallest mammal in Britain) are either dashing around like terrestrial blue bottle flies, or sleeping; there are no half-way measures for a shrew. Most only live for a year at most, which is hardly surprising given the rate at which they exist. Watching a day in the life of one of these creatures is the equivalent of watching two months of human activity.

WHERE AND WHEN

Though they are active throughout the winter, both species are far more obvious during the spring, summer, and early autumn. This is partly due to the populations being at their highest at these times, and partly as a result of behaviour.

The habitats most likely to harbour either species include deciduous woodland floor, hedgerows, gardens, sand-dunes, heathland; in fact, just about anywhere which provides some shelter and a constant supply of invertebrates to eat. The best habitat, from an observational point of view, is the floor of a mature deciduous forest that allows relatively clear views over a wide area. The pygmy shrews tend to prefer a more open habitat, such as hedgerows, though both overlap in their choice of home.

I have seen young shrews out of the nursery nests in late spring, mid-summer and early autumn, though two litters of young are the norm for most females. It is the last litter which is most likely to survive the rigours of winter to breed the following spring.

TRACK AND SIGN

What *could* such a tiny animal leave as a clue to its whereabouts? They don't eat nuts or any other seed, though they do sometimes eat a large number of snails leaving behind the chewed shells, but food remains rarely help with tracking. Their small shiny black droppings are scattered randomly and are very hard to find. The only sign that I have found at all regularly are their runs. These little tunnels may be either just below the surface of the soil, or more often, just between the soil surface and some overhead protection, such as dead leaves or some other vegetation. They are very hard to distinguish from the runs made by other small mammals such as wood mice and field voles, but the major difference is the size. A shrew rarely creates a tunnel any larger than the width of a man's finger, often smaller in the case of the pygmy shrews. Voles tend to leave chewed grass remains and droppings in their runs. The most common place to find shrew tunnels is underneath large flat stones or sheets of corrugated iron which have been lying on suitable ground. A swift lifting of such an object may well reveal a shrew scuttling around below (but be careful to replace the cover in precisely the same spot).

Where I used to walk as a boy in the woods near Bristol, I would often come across dead shrews in the middle of the track in the very early morning. By mid-morning they would all be gone, no doubt picked up by a passing crow or magpie. Just why this used to take place used to puzzle me enormously, until one morning, about an hour before dawn, I came across an immature common shrew, huddled in the centre of the path, unable to move. I picked up the tiny creature and tried to warm it in my hands, a beast so light that it was like holding a parcel of furry air, and there it died, unable to fight any longer. This must be the fate of a great many shrews, which, unable to find sufficient food to fuel their fiery metabolism, simply die of hypothermia and starvation overnight. The other common cause for finding apparently undamaged dead shrews is mammalian predators, particularly cats and foxes. These hunters often kill shrews, stimulated by their scuttling movements and squeaks, only to find that they taste disgusting. Shrews are rarely if ever eaten by anything other than owls and birds of prey.

SENSES

Shrews have quite good hearing, extremely poor eyesight, a good sense of smell and an incredible sense of touch. None of these, with perhaps the exception of hearing, will affect the field naturalist trying to get a view of one.

SOUND ADVICE

Shrews make a very distinctive sound, and though both the common and pygmy varieties call, the common shrew is much more vociferous. It is therefore fairly safe to assume that one heard calling in the field is either a water or common shrew. For some people, the calls are apparently too high-pitched to register, and I rue the day that I can no longer hear them, because the sound is an invaluable aid to location. The simple description of the calls would be to say that they are a high-pitched squeak, but this would be too simple to differentiate the sound from that made by any number of small mammals. To approximate the sound, start by saying: 'Tssip'. The 'Tss' sound is the basis of the mimicry of a shrew. Now try saying just the 'Tss' sound over and over, and slowly stop using your voice. You should be producing a very high whistling sound between your teeth. A shrew makes a call which goes something like 'Tss-ss-ss-sss-s, Tsss-s-sss-s-s-sss-s', and so on. The sound has a very metallic, almost ringing quality about it, and its distance in the field is often very hard to judge.

The only other sounds which may pin-point one of these little creatures, are mechanical ones—the quiet rustles and scrapes produced as they go about their foraging trips. Such noises may draw your attention to a shrew, but do not, in my experience, lend sufficient distinction to identify the animals without a sighting to confirm.

OBSERVATION

Almost all film and photographs of shrews will have been taken in sets (see Photography): spotting these tiny animals in the field is hard, and watching them for any length of time is practically impossible. This is simply because they are so tiny and spend so much of their time just below the cover of leaves and rocks, etc. I have managed to achieve wonderfully clear views of both species from time to time, but all occasions have been pure chance.

I usually respond to any sound which resembles that of a shrew by moving slowly and quietly towards it, keeping my eyes fixed on the point where any rustle or movement in the vegetation occurs. Shrews are sensitive to sound and will stop calling and sometimes freeze if you are too noisy in your approach. If you remain still, they sometimes come incredibly close, and I have had wild common shrews running over the palm of my hand.

PHOTOGRAPHY

The first bit of advice that I would offer regarding the photography of shrews is, don't. They are incredibly highly strung, difficult to manage, protected by law, and are very prone to dying in captivity, simply due to nervous exhaustion or starvation. But if you really want to try, the first thing you will need is a licence from the relevant conservation body in your area—English Nature, for example. This licence to photograph shrews will not be granted unless you can prove that you have experience in dealing with them. When I first started making wildlife films, this always struck me as something of a 'catch-22' situation, but in hindsight, it does sort out those people who are really serious about the pursuit and ensure some degree of welfare for the creatures in question. So, even before you get a licence, you will have to become familiar with trapping and handling shrews. The best way of achieving this is to join your local branch of the mammal society, where people who share your interest and who have experience in the field with all manner of species, will be able to show you the correct methods of trapping and handling them.

Spend time and care preparing the set in which they are going to be photographed or filmed. Shrews cannot jump very well but they can climb efficiently and move around like greased lightning. I have used all sorts of set designs to keep a small animal safely captive whilst at the same time achieve a clear view of it. A large aquarium will do, but elements which complicate matters with this method include reflections in the glass, condensation and flare from artificial lighting. A more effective glass enclosure can be made, based on a standard aquarium, but with the front set at an angle, facing down, so helping to eliminate some reflection problems. My own favoured method is to build a glass enclosure with the front panel missing. This is replaced by a 'nurse's sleeve' arrangement of fabric—literally a camera funnel on the front of a fish tank. There is absolutely no chance of unwanted reflections, and a well fitted, taped sleeve ensures there are no escapees half-way through a shoot. I find that zinc mesh netting, retained in a wooden frame, makes the best top to such an enclosure, allowing airflow whilst remaining secure.

Whatever the type of set you build (and mine seem to change and adapt for every new challenge), you must ensure that it contains all the elements to make life comfortable for its inhabitants. For shrews this means plenty of slightly moist soil, leaf litter, logs and rocks. These will give them places to explore and add to the authenticity of the set. It must also contain several dry areas which the animals can use as dormitories. I often create little nests of soft, dry grass within hollow logs or between rocks to provide them with plenty of choice. You must then ensure you have a good supply of food for them, and this will mean digging up worms, finding caterpillars, beetles and all manner of other invertebrates to satisfy their enormous appetites. A reasonable standby feed is bluebottle maggots and their pupae or casters, available from angling shops, and meal worms which can be bought in many pet supply stores.

Trapping a shrew involves the use of a live mammal trap, the best of which, and most widely used, is something called a Longworth Trap. Even these well designed bits of apparatus will kill a shrew unless used properly, either because of starvation or nervous exhaustion. The traps should be set along likely pathways, such as along the edge of logs, at the base of gate posts, along well established hedgerows, or any other natural funnel for activity. They should be fitted with ample dry bedding in the nest chamber and sufficient food for both rodents and insectivores. Food for rodents is easy to come by—a bit of apple and a handful of unsweetened muesli will do fine—but the trouble with most insectivore food is that it has a habit of wriggling away. The pupated stage of the blue bottle fly or meal worm beetle works well. Put at least ten pupae in every trap you set and ensure you visit the traps every two hours.

Once you find that one of the traps has been sprung, lift it gently from the ground, noting which trap you have, and where it was set, and blow gently at the door. This should send any little creature which is waiting just inside the tunnel retreating to the nesting box section. Now slowly open the door and try to see what you have caught. If you can clearly see that you have a species which you did not intend to catch, release it immediately in the same spot, allowing the creature easy access to cover. If, however, you cannot clearly identify the contents, take the whole trap (with door firmly closed again) to a place better suited for a thorough check. This is why it is so important to note where each trap was set, so that the animal within can be released as soon as possible in precisely the same spot it was first caught.

There are two ways of checking a trap's contents thoroughly. One is to empty the nest chamber into a clear plastic bag, and the other is to use a clean, dry, large dustbin as an emptying site. I prefer to use the latter wherever possible because it affords a clear view with minimal handling.

Assuming you have caught a shrew, if it shows any sign of stress (moving slowly or remaining completely still), release it immediately where you found it. This can sometimes feel like a waste of time, because the little creatures invariably scurry off into the undergrowth as if nothing at all were wrong, but the line between good health and dangerously high levels of stress with shrews is very fine indeed, and it pays to be extremely cautious with them.

If the shrew is moving around as normal and investigating its surroundings, transfer it as soon as possible to the set, put in suitable food and watch for at least an hour. A healthy happy shrew will feed almost immediately, forage around without spending inordinate amounts of time leaping at the edges of the enclosure, and probably curl up and sleep. If the animal you have caught does not feed and leaps repeatedly at the side of the enclosure, release it.

Plan to film or photograph the shrew within twenty-four hours of catching it. The longer you have the animal in captivity, the greater chance you have of stressing it.

I have found that both common and pygmy shrews usually settle very quickly into a well prepared set, and most appear to relish the room service and clean, dry bedrooms. They respond well to artificial light and quickly get used to odd noises, such as cameras clicking and whirring. Their activity cycle is such that a wait of three or four hours should produce plenty of views, though this depends to a certain extent on the amount of feed they get in each meal.

Don't put more than one shrew in the enclosure at a time unless you are completely familiar with their breeding behaviour; they are solitary creatures and can be very aggressive to one another confined within a small space. Do not keep the animals for longer than a day or two (often stipulated on the licence).

Do provide a small, shallow dish of water, buried so that the surface is at ground level, and ensure that there is no chance of the contents saturating the ground and chilling the shrew. *Do* check on the shrew at regular intervals; there is a fine line to be struck between keeping a careful note of the animal's welfare and disturbing it as a result of intrusive monitoring.

Water Shrew

(Neomys fodiens)

Though much of the behaviour displayed by this species is very similar to that of the pygmy and common shrews, there are a number of differences in its lifestyle and these warrant a separate section.

WHERE AND WHEN

With a name like water shrew, you would be forgiven for thinking that this species is found only by water. Not so. In fact, the best spot I know for them is in a deciduous woodland, where the only permanent water is a pond in the centre, and the shrews are often found a long way from it. They are superbly adapted for an aquatic life, however, with special fringes on their hind legs which help swimming, and a pelt which traps a layer of air for warmth when diving. From the point of view of observation in the field, there is no doubt that watery habitats are best, as elsewhere the shrews are as elusive as their more land-bound cousins.

They are most common around the south of England, though they occur over most of Britain, and I have had many excellent sightings of them hunting along the waterways close to our first house in Somerset. After two years with no sign of a water shrew, suddenly one summer they arrived. The first glimpse made me think I had spotted a new species of diving beetle, as the silvery layer of air which is trapped by the fur when the shrew swims beneath the surface belies its true, black-grey colouration. As this great beetle swam to the edge of the brook, hauled out and chewed on a fresh water shrimp, I realized my mistake. From that point on, for a period of about two months, we were treated to the company of these delightful animals foraging around the place. They spent most of their time hunting up and down the brook, occasionally slipping into our pond (which sat alongside the running water) and frequently scurrying about amongst the flower beds and dry-stone walls. Then one day they were gone, and we never saw them again in the two years we remained at the cottage.

Their daily activity cycle is quite predictable, apparently setting off to find food every three hours or so, and remaining very active for about half an hour, then slowly settling for another doze. I estimated that the 'troop' I watched consisted of about fifteen individuals, though I never made a thorough check. They certainly became active *en masse*, and would set the brook alive with their shrill whistling and scampering forms.

Like other shrews, this species remains active throughout the year, numbers taking a plunge during harsh weather. The most active period I have noted has been midsummer, from late May through to mid-July, and this period coincides with the emergence of the season's youngsters.

TRACK AND SIGN

Unlike their cousins, water shrews do leave one or two distinctive signs. The most obvious is their roosting and breeding tunnels which, in watery habitats, are often dug into the soft mud of the bank. The size of these burrows is critical to the wellbeing of the shrews, because the small diameter means the animals can only just squeeze through, and in so doing, expel moisture from their coats. Despite a fairly water-resistant pelt, water shrews do get saturated eventually, and without these tunnels would quickly chill and die. Any well-used hole in a river bank with a diameter, which is about the same as the width of man's thumb, will almost certainly have been made by this species. Some of the entrances to the tunnel system will be below the water's surface, and in clear streams and ponds these too may be visible.

Droppings can be found by closely scrutinizing every rock and log which sticks above the water's surface. They are very small and torpedo-shaped (no longer than 2 or 3 mm, much smaller than a water vole dropping), invariably black or grey, and may be deposited in large quantities on prominent sites. You may also find the remains of a meal on the same resting point, perhaps a few legs from a fresh water shrimp, or scales and a fin from a stickleback.

SOUND ADVICE

This is a particularly noisy shrew, and in my opinion, distinctive from its cousins. The basic sound is very similar to that made by a common shrew (see under preceding species), but differs in that it is a little louder, a touch lower in pitch, and more raucous and scratchy in quality.

SENSES

Though I am certain these little creatures hear well and have a keen sense of smell, they are quite indifferent to the nearby presence of a human observer. Their eyesight seems to be average or poor, typical of their family, but their sense of touch is well developed and used the whole time whilst foraging. They will freeze or move away if you move about noisily, or allow your shadow to be cast suddenly across them, but by and large they are very easy to approach and watch.

OBSERVATION

This is one of the very few species of small mammal which can be watched successfully in the field. The key to success is, as is the case with so many creatures, finding the right place. The best combination of elements is a narrow, slow-moving water course, with well vegetated banks and crystal clear water. Larger stretches of water offer the shrews a huge choice of hunting places, making it much more difficult to predict their whereabouts.

Once you have discovered a suitable site, spend the first few hours looking from a distance, getting some idea of the favoured pools, hauling-out points, and active periods. Having established these, you can get very close to a well-used area and sit quietly, waiting for the shrews to emerge. They will hunt within a few centimetres of your static form. It is also possible to watch them underwater, with the aid of a diving mask and snorkel. They are sensitive to sudden movement in these conditions and care must be taken to avoid this. Because much of their hunting seems to be done by touch underwater, it is possible for them to come very close to you, even investigating your submerged hands and feet.

PHOTOGRAPHY

Everything which applies to photographing the other species of shrew also applies to this one, only more so. It is possible, and very challenging to photograph this species in the wild with long focal length, close focusing lenses. But, like other shrews, the most effective way of photographing them is in captivity. They are protected by law, and you must be licensed to trap or keep them.

They are also difficult to care for, not just because of their nervous disposition and phenomenal appetites, but also because of their requirements for a tunnel system of precise dimensions. A set constructed within a waterproof enclosure, such as a large aquarium, is a reasonable starting point. You must be very careful to ensure that a good section of soil remains unsaturated for the shrews to dig their tunnels and dry off. One way of doing this is to set a waterproof container within a larger enclosure, and build up the land-based area around the pool. Feeding water shrews can be done in the same manner as the preceding species, and like them, each animal requires two-thirds or more of its own body weight in food every day. They will also appreciate access to aquatic foodstuffs, such as underwater invertebrates or small fish.

The Bats

(Chiroptera)

Bats are in many ways like flying shrews; they are largely insectivorous, they are very highly strung and sensitive to disturbance, and are all protected by law. Strictly speaking, you need a licence even to look at a roosting bat.

There are several species resident in the UK, each of which displays unique traits in hunting, roosting and hibernating. I have worked with five of the fifteen species which occur in Britain. Pipistrelle, long-eared, noctule, lesser horseshoe and greater horseshoe. Each is very different in behaviour and so I must assume that others, such as Daubenton's, whiskered, etc, are equally idiosyncratic.

Pipistrelle

(Pipistrellus pipistrellus)

If you see a bat, it is likely to be this species. Not only is it the most common in the British Isles, but it is also one of the smallest, and, from the naturalist's viewpoint, the easiest to watch. This is not simply because of its numbers but also because it is a good deal more hardy than many other bat species.

WHERE AND WHEN

Pipistrelles, or pips for short, turn up almost anywhere, from the far north of Scotland to the very southernmost parts of England, and right across Europe. They tend to have distinct roosts at different times of the year: a hibernation roost; another as a place where the females and younger animals congregate as a nursery; and isolated roosts used by the mature males for most of the summer. The sites chosen for hibernation tend to be deeper and better insulated than the summer roosts—large, hollow trees or the cracks between the mortar in large stone walls.

Most roosting sites are traditional and may be used for decades so long as no undue level of disturbance takes place. There may be a certain amount of movement between roosts during the course of the summer which may be explained by changes in temperature and availability of food. In the early spring, pipistrelles start to forage on the warmer evenings and form small gatherings, often just a couple of bats, in sites such as the spaces between roofing tiles or the narrow gaps behind unused window shutters. As the summer progresses the larger breeding roosts develop behind roofing tiles or other crevices in buildings, and it is here that the young are born and nursed, and that the greatest concentrations of bats occur. In one roost close to my home, there are usually well over 150 bats in residence every summer. These animals cram into the small gaps between tiles which clad the brick walls of a house, and up into narrow crevices in the roof space.

Some bats will also use regular night roosts—places where they stop to feed, groom and digest during the course of their nocturnal activities. Pips may return to their day roost or use any crack or gap they come across for this purpose. We have one bat around the cottage which always uses the space between the facia board and the wall, directly above our bedroom window, to eat large meals and digest others, and I have watched it on many evenings leave its roost next to the chimney, hunt for a while, then slip up inside its favourite resting place for ten minutes or so.

As summer wears on, the adult male bats, which have spent most of the year apart from the females, make their way to the nursery roosts to mate. By late autumn, the pips are starting to make their way back to their hibernating roosts, though a warm winter's day may still convince one or two, especially the younger animals, that it is worth venturing out for a quick, midwinter snack.

TRACK AND SIGN

Bats only leave a few clues to their presence: their droppings and their prey remains being the most common, and scratch marks at roost entrances are a good sign for some species.

Most bat droppings look very much the same to me, only differing slightly in size from species to species. The general look is of a small, torpedo-shaped, shiny black pellet, well tapered at both ends. Pipistrelle's dung is very shiny and 5 mm or 6 mm long. Clusters form beneath roosts, and if the bats are using a building, the droppings sometimes get caught on the walls and window sills as well as the ground below. A loft space will often reveal bat activity, and if the roost is a big one, the dung build-up can be considerable. I have never detected a heavy odour from any but the freshest bat dung. New deposits may have a hint of ammonia about them, though this scent comes more from the urine than the faeces, and soon dissipates. I am told it goes well on the garden and can even be used as an ingredient in gun powder.

Prey remains can be more diagnostic of a species. I have generally found pips to be quite clean feeders, rarely leaving any remains, apart from the odd small fly wing.

SOUND ADVICE

Bats produce ultrasonics—sounds which are above the range of human hearing, as a means of echo-location. They also, however, make lower-frequency squeaks and chatters which we can hear, and the mechanical sounds of flying and feeding may also attract attention.

Pips chatter a great deal just before they leave a roost, more so if they are uncomfortable with something outside, such as a human being standing too close. These calls tend to rise and fall in intensity, depending on the activity level of the animals, often reaching a peak when there is a traffic jam at the roost's exit. They are fairly shrew-like, but much more coarse and scratchy, delivered in a rapid chatter rather than a squeak. The mechanical sounds of a hunting bat are heard as a faint ticking sound, and are made both by the action of the wings and the emission of the ultrasonics.

One other sound, which I often hear is a vocalization made whilst in flight and which I can only describe as a contact call. Some species of bat do it much more than others (see noctule), and pips are one of those that do not do it much. It is very hard to describe, and many people I have been with in the field and pointed it out to have had difficulty discerning it even then. This turns out to be due to the quality of sound rather than its frequency, which is perfectly audible to most people. It is a short, metallic, ringing squeak, which sounds more as though it is coming from somewhere inside your head than from a little animal flying above. With pips, it is produced infrequently during the early period of emergence and rarely when they are hunting seriously. I always link it to a bat which is flying close to its roost site, or which has other bats of the same species flying nearby.

OBSERVATION

As you might expect, you need a licence to observe any species of bat in the roost; in fact, you need a licence to read a newspaper if you happen to be in an area where bats roost. This is not quite as silly as it sounds, because the nervous disposition of many bat species will not tolerate even the slightest suggestion that danger is lurking in the bedroom. From the bat's point of view, going to sleep is a very tricky time, because many go into torpor when they rest, and as such are completely unable to make a quick getaway if a threat suddenly appears. Your very presence may jeopardize the future of the colony.

As with shrews, it is best to seek advice from people already experienced with the observation of bats. Many local conservation bodies, have 'bat groups' affiliated to them, and these are a good place to start honing your skills and knowledge. These groups will also be able to recommend where to get equipment, such as a bat detector for use in total darkness.

The use of torches (with incandescent rather than fluorescent bulbs because of the high frequency whistle produced by many strip lights) is fine if it is kept to a minimum. Keep all visits to a roost quick and quiet, and do not re-visit a site too frequently.

Pips can be watched very successfully as they emerge from their roost, a period which provides some of the most exciting activity of their daily cycle. Arrive at the location an hour before dusk, settle to one side of the exit hole or holes, and sit rather than stand. This ensures your form does not present a large foreign body to the first bats that scan the area with their ultrasonics, and allows the free and natural exodus of the roost. Any walking close to the exit holes on your part will certainly hold up the normal course of events, and may, if the roost is not well established, convince the occupants that the site is unsuitable and cause them to abandon it.

Once pipistrelles have left the roost, they are quite difficult to watch in the dead of night. They will often fly quite early and return to the roost late, when there is enough light around in midsummer for a reasonable view, particularly against a western sky. They will even fly in broad daylight on rare occasions, a sight which is quite incongruous.

PHOTOGRAPHY

The nervous disposition and high metabolic rate of most bat species makes them far from ideal photographic subjects. Only when you are fully competent at watching these creatures should you begin considering taking stills or filming them and for this you will need a licence.

I have filmed bats both in the wild and captive states. The golden rules when working with these animals are to keep your visits or working periods short, silent and gentle. As soon as you enter an area where bats are roosting you are creating some form of disturbance; some animals will start to rouse from torpor, others may start chattering or even flying around. If it seems as though the colony is getting restless, it is time for you to leave.

With stills cameras or cine/video, pay special attention to the sort of lights you are using. Many flash guns and some other types of light produce ultrasonic whistles which can be enormously disturbing for a bat's sensitive hearing. Make sure that before using any form of lighting, you know what frequency of sound it produces (if any), and that it does not interfere with the bat's hearing range.

Whenever I work with bats in captivity, I never do so for longer than half an hour at a time, leaving two or three hours between sessions. This amounts to a total working time of one, to one and a half hours in twenty-four, and though this may sound like a short period, anything greater would risk overexertion of the little creatures.

In my studio in Somerset, I have created all manner of tunnels and sets for filming bats in flight, the most successful of which has been a narrow corridor made of black fabric with sacking at either end for the bat to settle on, and with the camera mounted on a track looking through a slot in one of the corridor walls. In this way I have been able to sweep along with the animal as it flies to and fro, using high speed cameras to capture the rapid movement.

Long-eared Bat

(Plecotus auritus)

Many of the details which apply to pipistrelles also apply to this species, but there are sufficient differences between the two to warrant a short section on the long-eared bat.

WHERE AND WHEN

Long-eared bats are much more solitary than pips, and those that I have come across have all been roosting in more open sites, such as cellars, dry-stone barns and large hollow trees. I have only ever found them in ones and twos, though I am sure they congregate in much larger numbers under certain conditions. My experience of their yearly cycle is limited, though they appear to follow much the same system as the pipistrelle.

The hunting technique of the long-eared is usually to glean prey from trees and bushes rather than capture it in open flight. This leads to a very acrobatic, fluttering flight close to foliage, with much stalling and hovering. They emerge late, usually well after dark, and return to the roost before the sky is light.

TRACK AND SIGN

Droppings from this species are a little larger than those from a pip, and typically contain a lot of remains from moths, especially wing scales. They are found under roosting sites and feeding perches, but I have never found them in very large volumes. Rest and digest perches, used during the night, are often identifiable by a litter of small to medium-sized moth wings on the ground below, one of the favourite prey items. These perches often occur in the roof space of open fronted buildings where disturbance is low.

SOUND ADVICE

They sometimes produce a chattering call in the roost, very similar to that of a pip.

OBSERVATION AND PHOTOGRAPHY

As one of the hardier bat species, long-eared are a good subject for watching. Their nocturnal habits can make observation in the field tricky, and even a bat detector can be of limited use due to the scarcity of loud ultrasonics produced. On a moonlit night, the flight silhouette of this species is unique, and due to the low hunting style and fluttering, sometimes hovering flight, if spotted it is very distinctive.

The long-eared bat has an average response to captive conditions and must be handled with great care. A licence is of course necessary for observation or photography but if handled properly this species will thrive for short periods in a studio set. I have filmed them in captivity, but kept all disturbance to a maximum of half an hour in every four or five.

Noctule

(Nyctalus noctula)

The largest common bat in England and Wales, it represents to me as much a harbinger of spring as the swallow, perhaps more so, because its activity is linked as much to the climatic conditions as to the season.

WHERE AND WHEN

I have seen noctules all over England and Wales, though never in Scotland, and in all sorts of habitats with reasonable access to large trees. Indeed, the smallest national reserve in the country that I know of is situated in a suburb and is no bigger than the base of a tree. This plays host to a well established noctule roost. The classic site for a summer roost of this species is a large tree, dead or alive, with an access hole leading to a hollow chamber. Despite being a relatively common species, these roosts are pretty hard to find given the high number of potentially suitable sites in some woodlands and hedgerows. In fact, the only way I know of finding them is to search all likely cavities, perhaps based on a general flight direction of animals leaving the roost at dusk, or returning at dawn. If you are really lucky you may hear squeaks and chatters coming from a hole at dusk as the animals rouse before emergence, or spot some dark residue from the base of a hole, caused by the noctule's droppings and urine.

Like many other bat species, the roosts which contain larger numbers of animals tend to harbour female and younger bats, whereas the adult males tend to roost singly, visiting the female breeding roosts in late summer and early autumn to mate.

This is certainly the easiest species to watch in the field, because it is often active very early in the evening, flying high, fast and direct over suitable hunting territory, darting after its insect prey from time to time. I have often seen good numbers hunting high over stretches of open water in midsummer, sometimes with Daubenton's bats, a species more usually linked with this habitat, foraging closer to the water's surface at the same time. Later in the night they tend to fly a little lower, with far less audible vocalization.

TRACK AND SIGN

Droppings are about twice the length or more of pipistrelle's, and all that I have found have been inside roosts. I have never seen this species using a feeding perch, only catching and eating all of its prey on the wing.

SOUND ADVICE

A very noisy bat this, its squeaks carrying across quite large distances and once recognized, often drawing attention to the animal's presence. The noctule produces a sibilant, ringing chirp much of the time it is in flight, a sound which is uttered in unison, though may have nothing to do with the ultrasonics the animals use to find their way around and hunt. Such a continuous stream of chit-chat might have some social contact role. The best evidence I ever had of this was one evening on the Somerset Levels, whilst watching ten or fifteen noctules hunting over a large lake. All the time I could hear the usual squeaks produced in the early evening flight. Through the centre of the hunting bats flew a black-headed gull, low and fast, obviously late for its roost. As the dark form of the bird passed among the bats, the usual rhythmic squeaks changed into a rapid trill, and the sound was very quickly adopted by most of the bats in the sky. Almost simultaneously, every one of them flew rapidly towards the ground, twisting and turning in a mode of flight which in birds is described as whiffling. A few seconds of silence followed, before the bats, one by one, resumed their normal flying and calling behaviour. For a while I was confused by the noctule's reaction to a harmless gull, until it struck me that they may well have mistaken the bird's form for that of a hobby, a raptor which regularly preys on bats in this part of the world. If this was indeed the case then what I had witnessed was a predator evasion tactic, aided by vocal contact.

OBSERVATION AND PHOTOGRAPHY

The greatest aid to spotting this species in the field is to recognize its call. Once you are familiar with the sound, hearing it will only tell you that there is a bat nearby, and not where the animal is in the sky. This is because the quality of the call is such that it is very hard indeed to establish the direction of its origin, and the best method for spotting the creature is to scan the whole sky rapidly as soon as you pick up the first hint that there is one about. Thereafter, use of binoculars suitable for poor light conditions will afford excellent views.

Though this is one of the hardiest bats in a captive situation, its size and flight style make it a difficult creature to care for properly. The only noctules which I have seen in captive conditions have been injured or sick animals which are being nursed back to health, or individuals which have access to good sized flight enclosures. I have never attempted to film this species in flight anywhere other than the wild.

Greater and Lesser Horseshoe Bat

(Rhinolophus ferrumequinum, R. hipposideros)

These are among the rarest bats which breed in the country, particularly the greater horseshoe which is endangered, due to its loss of habitat and its sensitive character.

WHERE AND WHEN

I have seen both species in a variety of locations when hunting, though associate them more with wooded country and farmland than any other. Like many bat species, the horseshoes have distinct summer and winter roost sites, the latter tending to be caves, mines and other large underground systems. In summer they both typically use the roof space of large buildings where disturbance is minimal and access is good.

TRACK AND SIGN

Lesser horseshoes can be found either singly or in quite large groups, and are often betrayed by the presence of droppings. These are about the same size as a pip's, though usually more brown than black. Rest and digest roosts are sometimes identifiable by the large number of crane fly remains found below them, a favourite prey item for this species.

Greater horseshoes leave large droppings, and are very obvious in the roost. Both species hang upside down whilst resting as opposed to squeezing into a crevice, and consequently are very easy to spot once a roost has been located. I have never knowingly found a greater horseshoe rest and digest perch, but the fact that they often return to the roosting site to groom and feed may help to explain this.

SOUND ADVICE

The only sounds I have heard coming from a lesser horseshoe have been mechanical, and my experience of greater horseshoes in the field is very limited. Of the roosts I have visited, all have been silent, but for mechanical flight and breathing sounds.

OBSERVATION AND PHOTOGRAPHY

The lesser horse-shoe is one of the most highly strung bats in the British Isles, and as such should be treated very carefully. During most of the summer, they slip into very deep torpor whilst resting, from which they can take up to thirty minutes or more to recover. Despite this, they will start to rouse at the first sign of disturbance, so all visits to a roost should be kept very short and sweet. This species very quickly suffers in captivity. Greater horseshoes are a little hardier, though fussy about their roosting requirements.

Both species, and any other bat, for that matter, can be photographed using high speed flash photography, incorporating infra-red beam breakers to trip the camera shutter release. There is some equipment commercially available which is suited to this method but most photographers who wish to work with very fast-moving subjects, like bats, end up having to design and have made the necessary gear. This sort of work requires as much innovative use of modern equipment as it does knowledge of the animals, but the results often reveal actions and behavioural quirks that were hitherto invisible.

The Brown Hare

(Lepus europaeus)

Hares can provide some of the most exciting mammal watching in Europe during the breeding season, and their antics have earned them a special place in folklore and mythology. My own work with hares has been concentrated around my Somerset home and, to a lesser extent, on the Wiltshire Downs.

WHERE AND WHEN

Brown hares prefer open grassland or arable land, especially where cover in the form of hedgerows and copses is plentiful. I have also seen them on heathland and in dense forest, but neither of these habitats is well suited to observation. The best time for hare watching is early in the spring. This is not simply because the animals are mating around this time (the breeding season extends throughout the summer, from January and February right through to September in good years), but primarily because the ground cover is at its lowest whilst the hares are sexually active. Dawn and dusk are peak activity times, but if a female hare is nearing oestrus (coming on heat), then chases and scuffles can break out at any time of day.

For most of the year, however, hares are primarily nocturnal, sitting tight in their forms during the day unless disturbed, and this is especially true of mothers suckling their young.

I have observed breeding behaviour as early as mid-February, and the latest matings I have seen have been at the end of July. These later sightings have either been made from an elevated position or else on fields which have already been cut once for silage or hay. I have filmed boxing in March (now there's a surprise), April and late June.

TRACK AND SIGN

The signs you are most likely to come across are runs, forms and droppings. The runs are most commonly found where the animals habitually make their way to or from cover, such as a woodland edge or through a hedge. The tracks usually evaporate shortly before and after these regularly used crossing points as the various animals spread out to feed on the more open ground. They resemble fox runs, and may even be used by both species, though those used exclusively by hares tend to be narrower.

Forms are the hare's daytime (and sometimes nocturnal) retreat, nothing more than a shallow depression in the grass most of the time, though I have come across a couple in arable fields which had been excavated to some extent, creating an oval dish-shape in the soil.

Droppings are very like a rabbit's, but usually larger and slightly more elongated. They are also scattered over a wide area and rarely in a concentrated heap as rabbits' so often are.

I have only come across hare footprints on a few occasions, mostly in soft mud where runs pass through hedges, and once or twice in snow. All that I have found have never revealed distinct toes, but rather rounded marks where the fore feet have met the ground in parallel, and long, club-shaped prints from the back feet, usually placed either side of or only just behind the fore feet. The only other species to make remotely similar prints is the rabbit, but the hare's hind foot measures at least 7 cm compared with the rabbit's 5 cm.

Their hair has a reddish base, black central portion and a tip varying from reddish brown to pale grey. It has cropped up in fields where the animals have been moulting or fighting and also on wire and bramble at crossing points.

Hares, like many large mammals, create dew paths in early morning, but these are very hard to distinguish from those made by other species.

SENSES

Hares use their superb senses of sight and hearing to detect danger. Though scent plays an important part in their social lives, it does not seem to serve a primary function in spotting trouble.

SOUND ADVICE

Unless stressed, hares are completely silent most of the time. During boxing bouts, the combatants grunt and wheeze, but this is only audible at very close range. A leveret or young hare which is stressed will produce a very shrill screech, similar to a rabbit scream, and mimicking this call may bring a female hare running up to you, presumably in defence of what she assumes to be her young.

OBSERVATION AND PHOTOGRAPHY

Undoubtedly the best way to watch hares is from a vehicle. If you can find suitable habitat which harbours a network of small roads or else gain permission from a land owner to drive a vehicle across pasture, the car acts as a superb hide and camera/binocular/telescope platform. Often all that shows of a resting hare is a narrow, dark, horizontal line in the grass. It is worth checking every dark or reddish blob which shows up in pasture, despite many being nothing more than dead grass or soil.

If you start your vigil early enough in the day and year, you should be rewarded with clear views of the animals as they forage before settling down to sleep. Watching at this time will also give you the opportunity to check for signs of breeding behaviour, and if these are evident, it may well be worth remaining in the area for the rest of the day. These signs are many and varied. The male hares will often check the ground for scent, walking in a loping and often zig-zag pattern, keeping their ears very erect and pointed to listen forward most of the time. Females coming into season lope casually about the fields, squatting occasionally and moving their tails from side to side, almost certainly leaving scent or pheromones as they do so. Where scent of an oestrus female is apparent, the males become excited and speed up their pace, frequently back-tracking when they momentarily lose the trail.

Once the female is located any number of events may occur. Most commonly, the male will sniff from a distance, then settle down to rest for the day in reasonably close attendance, waiting until the time is right. If another male is already in attendance, then a chase may ensue, the potential suitors sorting out who will have the right to mate with the jill (female hare). These chases may cover a huge distance, but I have never seen one end in a boxing bout between the males. In fact, the only contact I have seen between male hares has been a sort of nudging and thrusting with the front feet and head during a chase.

Boxing tends to occur when a male gets rather too pushy with a female who, though approaching oestrus, is not ready or willing to mate yet. Her response to an overenthusiastic suitor is to give him a good hiding, and boxing matches are usually a case of attack and defence rather than mutual attack. The male repeatedly attempts to manoeuvre behind the jill, who turns to fend off his advances.

It is possible to watch and photograph hares on foot, though you run a far greater risk of disturbing them. If the animals are involved in courtship they are sometimes blind to any other influence, a trait which may have added to their reputation of craziness. I have often had male hares run up to within a few metres of where I have been standing, and hardly shift to avoid bumping into me. Using hides in or on the edge of

Opposite: By ensuring you are upwind of a hunting barn owl you stand a good chance of the bird flying towards you, particularly when it is searching for prey among thin strips of rough ground along field borders.

Above: Red deer are at their most dramatic during the rut, when the stags find their voice. The use of a vehicle as a hide often works well with this species.

Above: They may be everywhere, but that doesn't make them easy to watch. Getting close to a mature wild rabbit presents a real challenge to the field naturalist, though this youngster is considerably less wary than its elders.

popularly frequented fields can pay dividends, though I prefer to maintain a wider view than a canvas hide allows.

If you manage to spot a hare in its form, then you may be able to approach it by using a rather silly-looking technique. At a distance, first move around so that you are broad side on to the animal. Then, at a quiet, level pace, walk towards it, ensuring that only one of its eyes can see you. As you move closer, bend your knees a little at first, then more so, and by progressively getting shorter you will give the impression to the hare that you are staying still (remaining the same size). There is a critical distance when sound and movement make it perfectly obvious that you are creeping up on the unsuspecting creature, and this differs from hare to hare, and the stealth of your approach. Once a hare has left its form, it may well circle around and try to approach its favoured site once again. Assuming you have moved to an acceptable distance and hidden well, this habit may well afford some good views.

Female hares are often extremely nervous when they are nursing young and must be treated with great care. The young are born above ground and are fully furred. They are left pretty much to their own devices for the course of the day. At dusk the females come to a regular spot where all the young gather for a very quick feed. A jill approaching this feeding place will not complete her journey if she feels there is the slightest chance of a threat nearby. Assuming all is clear, she makes the last few hops to the site in a wildly erratic manner, often covering large distances with each leap. I can only assume this is to scatter the scent of her trail should any ground predator be following. Suckling usually occurs when it is very dark, and on occasion during the night (I have only watched it in very late evening during early June).

Left: The sheer face of a warehouse provides kittiwakes with a perfectly safe nesting cliff. Even in the busiest urban centres, there are many natural wonders to be discovered.

The Mountain Hare

(Lepus timidus)

Though I have seen this species on many occasions in Scotland, I have never spent any time working with it or trying specifically to observe it. All sightings I have made suggest that it may be treated in much the same way as the brown hare, with perhaps more on-foot work because of its remote and often inaccessible choice of habitat. A quiet, well camouflaged 'watch-and-wait' in an area frequented by the species has worked well for friends of mine.

The Rabbit

(Oryctolagus cuniculus)

Though very common, rabbits represent a real challenge to the field naturalist, particularly the older, more experienced animals. Their traditional role as a game animal has instilled understandable and acute fear of all human activity.

WHERE AND WHEN

Since they were introduced to Britain by the Normans, rabbits have spread to every corner of the country. This ranges from sand dunes to heathland, indeed anywhere which includes areas of short grass suitable for grazing and plenty of dry ground in which to build their extensive systems of warrens.

Breeding occurs throughout the early spring and summer, the first females usually becoming pregnant in January and giving birth to several litters in a season. The courting male chases its mate in circles often resting his chin on the female's back before mounting. This species is most active during dawn and dusk, though some animals from a colony, particularly the younger ones, may be out and about throughout the day.

TRACK AND SIGN

Warrens are the most obvious sign of rabbits in the neighbourhood, but runs, prints, hair and dung are all indicators.

A rabbit hole is usually no larger than 50 cm across the entrance and often a good deal smaller. The burrows make up a network of interlinked underground runs which may extend over a very large area, with cropped vegetation around the warren and frequently a distinct variety of vegetation around the burrow entrances. This usually includes nettles and elder which thrive on the loose earth and high levels of nitrogen provided by the droppings. Some breeding burrows only have a single entrance which is stopped up with grass and hard to see.

The small, round or oval dung pellets are often clustered on top of mounds and bare patches of earth around the warren, but may also be scattered singly as the animals feed. They are green-brown to black in colour and usually smaller than a hare's, though size differs with the diet. An average is roughly 4 or 5 mm in diameter, compared to a hare's 6 or 7 mm.

Rabbits often scrape the soil to reach roots and tubers, and the little fan shaped digs are very distinctive. They usually measure 5 or 6 cm in length and 3 or 4 cm at the widest point. Runs through hedges and under fences are very like those of a brown hare, but are proportionately narrower and may well form a broken line where the animals regularly hop to or from a field. These hopping tracks may be worn smooth, each bare patch being roughly 30 cm apart. Footprints in soft soil or snow are like a smaller version of a brown hare's.

You may find tufts of hair snagged on bramble bushes or barbed wire fences, and this is very fine and soft, with a colour varying from sandy brown through to white. It is less coarse than the coat of a brown hare and you will find much less black in the middle of each strand.

SENSES

Hearing and eyesight are acute, but a rabbit's sense of smell plays little or no part in detecting danger. The rabbit's field of view is very wide, making it nearly impossible to sneak up on one unseen. Fast movement and even a static uncamouflaged human outline are both regarded as a great threat.

SOUND ADVICE

Rabbits are generally silent, the most common vocal sound being the distress scream, only produced when an animal is petrified, as when caught by a predator. They also produce a thumping sound by smacking their hind feet against the ground, and both of these noises serve as a warning to the rest of the colony that danger is near.

OBSERVATION AND PHOTOGRAPHY

The nervous disposition of most adult rabbits makes them very hard to get close to. Younger animals are far less wary and a quiet vigil on the edge of an established warren in spring or summer may well provide very close and intimate views of these. I have successfully used canvas hides and general body camouflage to get clear views of the adult animals, keeping all movement and sound to an absolute minimum.

Given the range and high population of this species, it is an ideal candidate for anyone wishing to practise their field craft and stalking methods. If you can get to within 5 or 10 metres of an adult rabbit, you're doing OK!

The Common Dormouse

(Muscardinus avellanarius)

The first thing to say about common dormice is that they are not common. Neither are they really mice, but members of a separate animal family. They are also extremely hard to observe in the wild, and because of their rarity are protected by law, so captive observations can only be done under licence. They are also charming, fascinating creatures that are well worth the effort involved in watching them.

WHERE AND WHEN

The other name for this species is the hazel dormouse, which offers a hefty clue to the type of preferred habitat. Hazel coppice was once common around Britain, but has become increasingly rarer in recent years. This may explain the scarcity of this little mammal over much of its former range. It is most common around the south and west of England, with a scattering of animals across mid and eastern Wales and one or two patches further north. Dormice can survive in other types of woodland and hedgerow habitat so long as there is sufficient food and a consistent leaf and branch canopy for getting about from A to B.

Food comes in the form of nuts, berries, flowers and pollen with the odd insect thrown in. The diet varies a great deal according to availability

throughout the year. Apart from hazelnuts, I have seen dormice feeding on ash keys, blackberries, honeysuckle flowers and sweet chestnuts.

This is an entirely nocturnal species; the only chance you have of seeing it in daylight is when it has been disturbed from its nest or else whilst it is still sleeping. This makes for very, very difficult observation, because the dormouse is so small that once in the leaf canopy it is completely invisible most of the time. It also hibernates from October through to April, but may move about earlier in the year if the weather is kind. All this does not lend itself to the ideal animal for observation in the field, and indeed all the filming I have done with this species has been in captivity.

TRACK AND SIGN

Given that the dormouse spends almost all of its active life climbing around the leaf canopy, there is little chance of finding any footprints, hair, runs or burrows (they do not dig). What you may find are feeding signs or nests to aid in tracking them down. The only food remains which can reliably be attributed to this species are hazelnut shells. Unlike mice and voles, dormice leave a very smooth, almost polished look to the inside edge of the small hole they gnaw in the shell. It looks almost as though someone had found a nut opened by a mouse, then, with a file or fine sandpaper, rubbed all trace of teeth marks from the inside of the hole. Around the outside edge of the hole there are many gouges made by the teeth, and these tend to be rather broader than those made by other species.

As far as nests go as a sign, I have only ever come across a few which have been built outside tree cavities or nest boxes. These were all made from fine strips of honeysuckle bark and lacked any sign of an entrance hole. Two that I came across in the same coppice were at about chest height in a tangle of bramble, and each was about the size of a grapefruit.

SENSES

Dormice have very good hearing and good eyesight, both of which are put to constant use in the vigil for danger. I do not think scent plays a major part in spotting trouble.

SOUND ADVICE

These creatures are very quiet in everything they do. They wheeze a bit when they are coming out of hibernation and they are reputed to make the odd squeak when they are courting, though I have never heard this.

I do not know how much work, if any, has been done on the possibility of this species using very high-frequency squeaks, but my observations of captive animals would suggest they may be more vocal than we think. A good candidate for the use of a bat detector perhaps?

OBSERVATION AND PHOTOGRAPHY

Because this species is so difficult to observe in the wild, most behavioural observations have been made with the help of radio telemetry (a tiny transmitter on the animal sending out pulses which can pin-point its position with the use of receiver) or with animals in captivity. Dormice readily take to nest boxes which can help a great deal when it comes to searching for their sleeping quarters. The ideal design is built along the same lines as a blue tit nest box, but with the hole facing the trunk of the tree instead of outwards. A couple of small blocks of wood between the tree and the box ensure the dormice can gain access. I have found four or five animals all sleeping in the same box, and have heard reports of many more doing so.

Disturbance or handling of these creatures is not permitted without a licence. They do very well in captivity so long as the correct food, bedding, and water are provided, though are not all that easy to watch even then. One of the ways dormice avoid being eaten is to ensure they do not make any noise, and they achieve this by freezing if they hear or detect what they think is danger. In the quiet of a studio this can be incredibly frustrating, as the click of a shutter release or the whirr of film passing through the camera are sufficient to put a dormouse into freeze mode for ages. They seem to be much more relaxed if there is some ambient noise around which may help cover the sound of their movements, particularly constant rustling sounds like wind in the trees. This has to be one of the very few creatures which is easier to watch when its surroundings are noisy; I have found that a cooling fan blowing on to a branch of dried leaves creates the ideal sound.

I have filmed dormice in all manner of set designs, the most successful of which has been a sort of corral made out of perspex, about 60 cm high and 3 metres or so in diameter. In the centre I construct a set using living hazel, bramble and so on, making sure none of the branches overhangs or comes within a metre of the sides. Because dormice are relatively poor at leaping, they are unable to clear the height of the smooth-sided corral, and spend most, if not all, of their time foraging around in the branches. I generally limit the time spent working with this species to an hour or so at a sitting, though if an individual is obviously very relaxed, this can be extended. Indeed, some get very bold the more you habituate them to your movements and sounds.

The Water Vole

(Arvicola terrestris)

This was one of the first wild animals which I spent any great amount of time trying to watch. Sadly, the population which I cut my field-craft teeth on is no longer present, due entirely to pollution. This fate has befallen many other populations of water vole so that they are now much less prolific than they once were.

WHERE AND WHEN

This species occurs right across England and Wales and parts of Scotland, usually along lowland freshwater habitats. They are active throughout the year, the best time to watch being mid to late summer when the populations are high and social activities common. It is also the time that many fisheries cut the aquatic weed from their beats, and this provides a floating banquet for the voles which drift downstream on the great rafts, eating as they go.

I have seen voles out and about at all times of the day and night, early morning being a favourite, and at regular intervals thereafter. Each vole seems to stick to its own timetable, and even in areas with high populations, there are rarely more than two or three out at the same time. This is probably just as well, because during the breeding season, which extends throughout most of the summer, adults of the same sex are very aggressive towards each other.

TRACK AND SIGN

Footprints are similar to a rat's, though much more spread out and star-like. The front foot displays four toes and is often partly covered by the print from the hint foot which has five toes. The droppings, which are about a centimetre long and dark brown or green, particularly if you break them open, often form piles on prominent rocks or logs poking out of the water, or on the bank close to a tunnel entrance.

They dig a complex system of tunnels into the soil of the bank with entrance holes above and below water level, as well as some leading into feeding areas on the bank itself, sometimes quite a way from the water's edge. The holes measure about 5 or 6 cm across, and in active tunnels there is frequently a lot of fresh spoil left beneath the entrance. These tunnel systems may remain long after the animals that built them have disappeared.

Runs are created through bankside vegetation, and are distinctive by virtue of their smooth base and diminutive size, rarely any wider than a man's hand.

SENSES

Voles have reasonable hearing when out of the water and good eyesight when trying to spot movement, but they are not good at picking out inanimate forms.

SOUND ADVICE

They are usually very quiet, but during the fights and other social interactions I have watched, there has been a lot of shrill squeaking and chattering.

OBSERVATION AND PHOTOGRAPHY

In areas where they are common, water voles are relatively easy to watch and photo-graph. Look for an animal which regularly uses the same place to feed or groom, and wait for it to pop back into its tunnel. As soon as it is out of sight, carefully walk into a position which will afford a good view of the favoured spot, and with luck you will be treated to some very intimate views. Once the vole is out it is essential that you remain motionless; the slightest flick of a head or hand will almost certainly send it scuttling for cover. At very close proximity the sounds of cameras will have to be muffled.

Other Voles Mice and Rats
(Muridae)

This is a very broad heading to deal with a number of other species for which the observation and photographic methods are similar. It includes wood mice and yellow-necked mice, field and bank voles, as well as house mice and brown rats.

WHERE AND WHEN

All of these animals are active throughout the year, and many share roughly the same calendar. All are capable of raising several litters of young through the summer, and some can breed all through the year, nesting conditions and food permitting. This is particularly true of the species associated with man, such as rats and house mice. The summer and early autumn months always see the populations peak, and are the best times for watching or live trapping these animals. Mice and rats tend to be most active during the night, whereas voles are active at periods throughout the day also.

Certain habitats are preferred by some more than others. Wood mice, as their name suggests, are prolific in deciduous woodlands, though their catholic tastes mean a wide variety of other types of country are used, from fields and hedgerows to railway embankments and suburban gardens. Field voles are animals of grassland, whereas their cousin, the bank vole, is more likely to be found along well established hedgerows and woodland.

TRACK AND SIGN

All of these small mammals leave certain distinctive clues to their whereabouts. Let's start with hazelnut remains. The wood mouse and yellow-necked mouse both gnaw a hole in the shell, leaving many scratches and tooth marks on the outside edge of the hole, and a well marked inner lip. Bank voles also attack these nuts by chewing a hole, but leave hardly any mark on the outside edge. Field voles do not often eat hazelnuts, concentrating instead on grasses, but those that I have offered a nut to in captivity have left a sign similar to that of a wood mouse, but with rather neater tooth marks on the outside edge, positioned very close to the lip of the hole. I have never found hazelnuts which I could be sure had been eaten by rats (squirrels split hazelnuts down the middle).

Wood mice especially will make caches of uneaten food underneath logs, bits of old corrugated iron, indeed anywhere which offers suitably dry cover. These may contain just a few, or large numbers of nuts, seeds and any other food which will keep. Often the remains of already eaten meals are amongst the litter, providing a further clue to the hoarder's identity. I have never found caches which belonged to bank or field voles apart from grass stems attributed to the latter. Rats and house mice tend to feed wherever they locate a meal instead of carrying it away.

All droppings from this group of animals look similar. Size varies from a centimetre or so long in brown rats, on a descending scale, which follows this order: brown rats; black rats; water voles; yellow-necked mice; wood mice; field voles; bank voles; and finally house mice. The colour varies according to the meal, but field voles usually produce very green droppings because of their grass diet, and mice all produce predominantly black faeces. Most are quite scentless to our noses, with the distinct exception of those of the house mouse, which produces a characteristic, musty smell. Brown rats and field voles generally deposit their dung in collective sites, unlike most other small rodents which scatter them randomly.

Footprints are all four-toed on the front foot, five-toed on the back, and follow roughly the same size scale as the droppings. The prints you are most likely to encounter are those made by rats and water voles in soft, waterside mud. Both are very similar, with the print made by the front feet usually covered in part by those of the back feet.

Other signs are runs, smear marks (produced by house mice and rats along horizontal walkways in buildings), urine pillars (produced where house mice repeatedly urinate in the same place and a mass of sticky dust and urine collects, bearing the distinctive house mouse scent), and general gnawing at a myriad of objects from antlers to aluminium. Many of these signs are very similar for several of the species, though field voles often create a little lawn of distinctively gnawed grass stems around the entrance to their burrows and along runs.

SENSES

All of these animals respond to movement and sound, but do not appear to use their noses to detect danger.

SOUND ADVICE

Most of these animals squeak, and some squeak louder than others. House mice and brown rats are particularly vociferous.

OBSERVATION AND PHOTOGRAPHY

As you might expect, most observations and photographs taken of these animals are done in captivity. Out of the whole group, brown rats are perhaps the best suited to watching in the wild, particularly where populations are very high and concentrated around a known food supply, such as a grain store. You can bait an area of woodland with peanuts and then watch it at dusk, perhaps with the aid of a dim torch, but the best you are likely to see are the brief flashes of mice or voles as they nip in, grab a nut, and dash away again.

If you live in an area which has some of these creatures in the garden, a small mammal feeding-station can provide good views. This can be a simple platform, with a tunnel or ramp leading out of an area with thick cover and up to the table for the mice and voles to gain access, or perhaps a more elaborate box, attached to a downstairs window of the house, with an open side against the glass. Access to the box is also gained via a ramp or tunnel. Remember to provide lots of toe-holds: plastic plumbing pipe is too slippery unless you cut lots of narrow holes, like a ladder, along the base. Bait the area around the opening to the tunnel with nuts and grain and provide a meal in the box itself, and with luck you will be rewarded with visits from a mouse or vole, who may well spend some time feeding in the box.

Captive viewing is the most successful method, and though you do not need a licence to trap these animals, you should of course treat them with the same degree of care as you might afford to a more sensitive species. The use of Longworth Traps (see the section The Shrews) is the usual trapping method, and like shrews, the same precautions for the animal's welfare should be taken. A cereal mixture including nuts and grains will keep all members of this group healthy for several hours in the trap. Once caught, it is important to remember that many of these animals can jump extremely well, and losing one away from its usual habitat and territory may be condemning it to death. Take every precaution to prevent this happening, including a secure, gnaw-proof set or enclosure for the duration of the animal's stay.

All of these animals get used to artificial light quite quickly, though will prefer to feed in the shadows if allowed. When using bright filming lights, I limit their use to prevent the sensitive eyes of the mice and voles becoming too dry.

The Red and Grey Squirrel

(Sciurus vulgaris, S. carolinensis)

Both the grey and the much rarer red squirrel follow similar lifestyles, and both are accessible to the field naturalist, being primarily diurnal. They are also among the most appealing of mammals, and watching their acrobatics in the tree tops is a real treat.

WHERE AND WHEN

Red squirrels are now relatively scarce in Britain compared with the populations here 100 years ago. This decline cannot be directly attributed to the arrival of the North American grey squirrel to the country, because the red was already in decline before the newcomer spread. It does, however, seem likely that where numbers of red squirrels have decreased through disease or other factors, they may be hard pressed to make a recovery in areas where the grey squirrels have been able to fill their niche. The best places to watch red squirrels are across the forests in the centre and east of Scotland, on some of the off-shore islands in the south of England, specifically Brownsea and the Isle of Wight, and in one or two patches of East Anglia, Wales, and across much of Ireland.

This species tends to prefer mixed conifer forest or a blend of conifer and deciduous trees. I usually associate them with Scots pine, but on Brownsea have seen them using oak as much as any other tree, both for feeding and building nests.

Grey squirrels were first introduced to Britain in the late nineteenth century, since when they have spread to most forested parts of the

country as far north as Liverpool, with isolated populations in the border country and eastern Ireland. Part of their success as a species can be explained by their wide choice of habitats: as well as deciduous and mixed forest, they are just as comfortable in mature hedgerows, parks, and gardens, so long as there are sufficient mature trees and foodstuffs to meet their needs.

Both species are diurnal, though I have, on very rare occasions, seen a squirrel out and about on a moonlit night. The peak of activity tends to occur shortly after dawn, with further active periods every two or three hours. Red squirrels, in particular, are very busy around first light.

Most mating I have seen has taken place in the late winter, early spring (February and March are always good months to watch courtship). Squirrels may raise two litters of young in a season, mating again in the late spring and giving birth in summer. All the squirrels I have watched have reared one family a year, but not all in the same season. The peak time for seeing young is usually around April and May, with another batch of mobile young, though often fewer, in the trees in early autumn.

Clearings which have a lot of fallen food, such as beech mast or acorns lying on them, are all good places for sitting quietly and watching squirrels. Some get so used to people that they will readily take food from the hand, more so the grey than the red in my experience.

TRACK AND SIGN

I have found squirrel footprints in snow and in soft mud on the woodland floor. The toes and pads are often quite distinct, with the longer, five-toed hind print invariably just in front and to the sides of the smaller four-toed fore print. The toes look quite spidery and well spaced, with the claw marks often showing. The whole effect is a little like a tiny rabbit print, but with much clearer toe definition.

I have come across squirrel droppings, often on tree stumps which have been used as a feeding station, and these look like a large rat dropping—torpedo-shaped and greenish brown in colour. Like most other dung, the colour is affected by the diet.

Both red and grey squirrels deal with fir cones in a similar way, biting off the scales to reach the seeds beneath and leaving a characteristic 'corn-on-the-cob' effect, with only the topmost scales remaining on the otherwise bald core. Hazelnuts are split with a well positioned bite on the seam, creating the neat, two-half shell remains that are so commonly found on the woodland floor. Immature squirrels are less proficient at this than adults and may leave some gnaw marks and a ragged edge to the split, but no squirrel ever chews a hole in a nut shell.

A wide variety of other foodstuffs are eaten, from sweet chestnuts, which are prised from their prickly cases, to birds' eggs and nestlings on occasion. Squirrels will sometimes enlarge the hole of a cavity nest, whether it is in a natural site or a nest box, to gain access to the bounty within, or perhaps to use the hollow as a dray. The marks are obviously created by teeth as opposed to the pitted look created by a woodpecker.

Drays (nests) may be built within hollows but are more usually bulky structures of stripped bark, moss and leaves, often very high up in the cleft of branches or, in the case of conifers, where a pair of branches meet the trunk. Most are at least the size of a football, many are larger. They all have a more or less spherical form and lack any obvious entrance hole. The very similar magpie nest rarely has as much leaf material and bark included, and the bower which encloses the top of the nest is a loose structure with clear openings to the nest itself visible from the sides.

Where a squirrel has stripped the bark from trees for nest building, particularly sweet chestnut and maple, a distinctive frayed, ragged look to the affected area remains. Most of this sort of work is done in the very early spring. Squirrels also strip bark from trees at other times of year to get at the nutritious layers just beneath, and sometimes the damage caused is so great that the tree dies.

Food caches are made but you are very unlikely to find these, because they are buried randomly just beneath the surface and contain only one food item in each. The popular concept that this behaviour only occurs in the autumn is due simply to the squirrel's habit of reacting to any food glut by storing what it cannot eat immediately, and this, of course, is only likely to occur in the wild during the autumn months, when the mast from many tree species is ripe. A handful of peanuts, proffered in midsummer, will have precisely the same effect, compelling the squirrels to indulge in a bout of burying.

SENSES

Squirrels have excellent eyesight and good hearing, both of which are used the whole time in the search for danger. Movement is spotted much more readily than colours or form. Smell does not play such an important part in this role, though is very well developed in social interactions. A squirrel which is about to exit a dray, and which manages to spot you and so goes back inside, can be tricked if you move your position by a few yards whilst the animal is out of sight. The next time it pokes its head out to look for danger it will stare directly at the point it saw you last, and so long as you are reasonably well camouflaged and perfectly still, will emerge into the open

SOUND ADVICE

Both species produce a wide range of hoarse coughing and wheezing calls. When a red squirrel spots danger, it makes a sound which sounds like 'chuck ... chuck ... chuck'. I have also heard them produce a more gentle wheezing sound during low intensity social contact. Mating chases are accompanied by a wide range of calls along the same lines as the alarm note.

Greys have a vocal quality not dissimilar to that of a magpie; indeed, I well remember thinking the first one I ever heard producing an alarm call was a magpie with a sore throat. The hoarse, wheezing sound is quite easy to mimic, by using a nasal pitch in your voice, and saying something like 'Ha ... Ha ... Ha ... Heaaaaa'. This sound is often repeated over and over, and can be a good indicator of a hidden predator nearby. I have found many roosting tawny owls and one or two foxes by following the gaze of a squirrel which was making an alarm call, but be aware that the predator causing the alarm might be you.

OBSERVATION AND PHOTOGRAPHY

Most squirrels tend to go where the food is, and this habit can be worked to your advantage. By establishing a feeding station in the centre of a woodland where squirrels are common, you may well be able to predict their antics throughout the day. Pick a natural site, such as the top of a tree stump, to put out the food—peanuts are always a good staple diet. Most insectivorous birds should be avoiding nuts in summer, but to be sure that you do not cause any young birds to choke, it is best to restrict the use of a 'squirrel table' to the late summer, autumn and winter months. Put up a hide within 10 metres of the platform and after about a week of constant feeding, make your first watching visit. Arrive early, before first light if possible, and put some food on the table as usual. Squirrels should start to arrive very soon after first light, though you may well be surprised by some of the other visitors. My squirrel tables have been visited by wood mice, jays, foxes and badgers!

The problem with this sort of observation is that the only behaviour you are going to witness is feeding and a bit of argy-bargy when more than one squirrel is at the site at the same time. For views of more natural activity you have to be mobile, walking carefully though the woodland, eyes trained skyward for any movement in the canopy. Most squirrels will see you before you see them, and depending on their experiences of mankind, will either freeze, dash away or jump down on to your shoulder to see if you have any goodies on you. In all but the most habituated populations the first two reactions are most common. An unmoving squirrel can be very tricky to pick up, especially as they tend to do this on the blind side of a tree trunk. If you suspect a squirrel is in a tree but cannot see it, gently walk away, trying to keep your face averted, but all the time checking for movement. With luck, the animal will relax sufficiently to venture out before you have gone too far. If it does not, walk on and return to the site from a different direction.

Section 3

The Birds

Birds are probably the most accessible form of wildlife right across Europe. By this I mean you can wander out with a pair of binoculars virtually anywhere and see a bird doing something interesting, in broad daylight. This may well explain why bird watching and the accompanying plethora of literature about the subject are so popular.

As with the section on mammals, I will not attempt to describe how to identify species in the field; nor will I attempt to point out where you may go to see them, or at what time of year, there are many other terrific books available that more than adequately fulfil this role. In the following section I shall attempt to fill in some of the more specific gaps which may have been left out of some identification guides, with a particular emphasis on field craft, tips and photographic techniques. I will also avoid too much detail on how to go about finding nests. Though this can be a very valuable element in field craft, it is knowledge which I am afraid may be abused by those few in search of eggs or nestlings, and for the purposes of this book at least, have chosen to omit it.

Rather than deal with each species individually, I shall deal with each 'group' of birds as a whole, referring to individual species where it aids clarity.

One of the most fascinating and frustrating elements of bird watching is the enormous variety of species you may encounter in a single day. It soon becomes apparent that the more time you spend in the field, the more birds and other animals you see, and not by accident. As your ability to pick up little signs and spot clues that are hidden to most develops, you almost imperceptibly accrue an enormous fund of knowledge and understanding that soon becomes an indispensable element of your bird watching skills. Indeed, looking back, it may well be hard to imagine how you ever spotted a sparrowhawk or kingfisher without it. It is impossible to separate these clues to identify distinct species. Whereas a call note may be the single most important clue for spotting one species, it may be the guano (droppings) or feeding remains of another that give it away.

When dealing with close observation and photography, the bird's character (nervous, hardy, etc) will be described as well as methods of hide introduction, etc.

Divers and Grebes

(Gaviidae, Podicipedidae)

Because these birds stick to a watery habitat, there are few special tricks to spotting them; just scan with your bins and you will see them swimming and diving occasionally. There have been many occasions when my attention has been drawn to a red-throated diver by its eerie call drifting across the waters of a Scottish loch. They also produce a distinctive croaking flight call which catches the ear and draws the eye. Most of the views I have had of black-throated and great northern divers have been during the winter, when the birds are generally more quiet but for the occasional wailing cry which never lasts very long, and is often all but lost in the sound of sea wash.

To photograph any diver on the nest in the British Isles you must first obtain a licence from English Nature. These birds are generally quite nervous and must be treated with great care when incubating eggs. Use of a hide is essential, and this should be introduced slowly, preferably over a period of days.

The two species of grebe most common in the UK—great crested and little—are both widespread and easy to spot on the lake or pond they inhabit. They leave no clues to their whereabouts, spending almost all of their time on the water. In areas which have densely vegetated banks and reeds, little grebes may be difficult to spot due to their more skulking nature, but are often betrayed by their manic, liquid trill of a call. Great crested grebes are less vocal, but do produce loud braying calls during the breeding season. I have successfully drawn this species close to the bank by mimicking this sound, but found that they quickly grew bored when no visual contact with their supposed antagonist was made.

The courting behaviour of this species is one of the most spectacular displays in the bird world, but due to the nature of the bodies of water preferred—usually larger lakes—it often takes place some distance from the bank. For closer views, look for long, thin lakes which will permit a reasonably close view of the birds wherever they are on the water. They often choose to conduct displays just after boundary disputes with neighbouring pairs, a sort of pair bond confirmation, and these tiffs may

well take place time and again in roughly the same place. By hiding reasonably well on the bank opposite such a site, you should be treated to excellent views.

Both species build their nests among emergent water vegetation or branches which dangle into the water. Though the nest platform may be clearly visible, it is more often partially or completely obscured by the surrounding greenery. It is a simple matter, however, to watch these birds return to the nest when sharing incubation so long as they do not suspect any danger. They both respond well to the introduction of portable hides, and all the birds that I have filmed have accepted my presence within half an hour of putting up the canvas.

Petrels, Shearwaters and Fulmar

(Hydrobatidae, Procellariidae)

These entirely sea-going birds are all great masters of the air. Even the tiny, frail-looking storm petrels travel for thousands of miles over the most treacherous waters. I have found and watched fulmar and manx shearwater on the nest in Europe and other species of tube nose in the Antarctic.

Spotting any of these birds whilst they are out at sea is a matter of dogged perseverance with a telescope and a flask of coffee. By positioning yourself on a headland which juts out well away from the mainland, you stand a much better chance of picking them out. Such places are usually well known by experienced 'birders' and after some stormy autumnal weather are often bristling with scopes and tripods owned by bird-watchers keen to catch a glimpse of a passing wayward rarity. Keep a keen eye on any dark shape which pops above the peak of a wave then disappears, as most of these birds are uncannily good at flying just above the water's surface, despite massive seas. In fact, they often use the action of the falling waves on the surrounding air to help keep them airborne.

Many of these birds only visit their nests to feed chicks during the hours of darkness, largely because of their complete incompetence on the ground. Having landed, their waddling gait makes them easy prey for passing gulls and skuas, and many are preyed on despite this nocturnal habit. Shearwaters and petrels can be quite accepting of humans around the nesting sites at night, though this differs enormously among populations and great care must be taken when dealing with an unknown group. They do not take too kindly to lights being shone on them as they approach their nesting burrows, though once on the ground, can be observed with a dim torch. Once in the burrow (shearwaters and smaller petrels all use tunnels in the ground as nesting chambers), they seem to accept a small amount of artificial light so long as it is introduced slowly. Most work I have done with these birds at night has incorporated the use of image intensifiers and infra-red lights which have no effect on behaviour. I have even had them land in my lap (and on my face)!

Unlike their cousins, fulmars are cliff-nesting birds, relying on the inaccessibility of their site to deter predators. For field naturalists and photographers, the deterrent effect is just as successful: dangling off a cliff by a rope to get a good view is something you do not do lightly. There are, however, sometimes spots along cliffs where a headland juts out and whose face is clearly visible from the opposite crest. Such locations are often favoured by the fulmars and make ideal observation points. So long as the adult birds are confident you are not able to reach the nest, they will return with impunity even if you remain in full view. If you are adventurous or foolhardy enough to attempt to reach a nest, then beware the oily substance which all fulmars, chicks included, are capable of vomiting with great accuracy into the face of a supposed threat. Quite apart from being pretty shocking, the effect is enduring as the oil carries a scent which is both potent and revolting.

Fulmars can be a good indicator of other coastal inhabitants, specifically predators. As they glide back and forth along the cliffs, they will check their flight and look down, often repeatedly, if they spot something that they perceive as a danger. This behaviour has led to my spotting all manner of creatures, from peregrine falcons and sea eagles, to otters.

Cormorants

(Phalacrocoracidae)

Both cormorants and shags are plentiful around the coasts of Europe, especially where high cliffs can provide their favoured nesting sites. As a water bird, the method used for spotting them is again quite simply a scan-and-search with binoculars or a telescope across the surface of the sea, loch or lake they are using. On the still waters of Scottish sea lochs an outline and ripple can often make your heart leap, because, at first glance, it can be mistaken for the effect made by an otter. This is particularly true of hunting birds which often swim very low in the water, with their faces submerged in search of prey. On choppy water at sea, their diving action may catch the eye and also give you a few moments of anguish until they surface and reveal their long neck, and with it their identity. Hunting birds are fairly wary of a human form waiting on the bank nearby, and may well drift away once they have spotted you. This is naturally more evident in areas where they have been shot at due to their predations on fish stocks. That said, a friend of mine who runs a salmon farm in west Scotland often has a shag perched on the floating pontoons, capitalizing on the many smaller fish which congregate below the nets, whilst the salmon are being fed. There is no doubt that cormorants and shags learn quite quickly who they can trust.

On the nest both are nervy, and any close observation requires a hide in all but the most remote or well habituated populations. Each colony and individual reacts differently to human beings, based on their experience.

Cormorants occasionally nest in trees next to inland fresh water, and these colonies are made extremely obvious by virtue of the copious amounts of droppings which eventually damage and even kill the nesting trees.

Gannets

(Sulidae)

This is a sea bird and a half. Big, dynamic, and beautiful, they nest in vast colonies on well established sites. Many gannet colonies are well known and well watched, made all the more simple by most of these birds' relative indifference to human presence. This is another species that, with care, can provide excellent views with minimal preparation. Most, if not all, of the large colonies are protected by conservation bodies and you must seek permission before attempting to reach them. For very close observation, use of a hide may be advisable with some groups of birds.

Gannets hunt in the open sea, plunge-diving into shoals of fish in what can only be described as an impossible break-neck manner. A certain method of watching the feeding behaviour is to be on, or follow, a fishing vessel, particularly a trawler, which may well be followed by a cloud of sea birds, including gannets, looking out for an easy meal of fish guts or spilled catch. When they get into the rhythm of a good feed, gannets virtually ignore everything else around them and it is possible to get some very close and dramatic views from a boat.

Herons

(Ardeidae)

My experience with European herons has concentrated on the grey, with some work on bitterns, night herons and egrets. These skilled hunters have uncannily good eyesight, and, depending on their attitude to human beings, this can make them pretty hard to watch.

Grey herons are fairly common in the UK and can be seen hunting on virtually any body of water, from coastal estuary to garden pond. Their distribution and habitat vary throughout the course of the year. They nest communally during the spring and summer, and so are bound to fish on waters within striking distance of the heronry. Early in the year, from February onwards, they start to arrive at these traditional nesting areas and re-establish building sites. Most heronries are situated in the tops of tall trees, often within a small copse or on the edge of a larger wood. Occasionally they nest singly, and these lone pairs can be very tricky to pin down. At this time, and throughout the incubation period, which for some birds may last up until late June, the adult herons are quite inconspicuous, often hunting in the early dawn and late evening, and just enough to satisfy their own appetites. As the summer wears on, the adult herons become increasingly active in order to satisfy the growing appetites of their now hatched chicks, and will hunt throughout the day, often gathering in areas where the feeding is good. Getting clear views of this hunting behaviour can be achieved in a number of ways, but all depend on a degree of stealth and hiding as all but the most well habituated of herons are nervous birds.

One of the most successful techniques is to use a vehicle as a hide. This method is best suited to habitats where a road system is frequently flanked by suitable hunting grounds, such as the Somerset Levels or parts of Norfolk and Suffolk, and indeed where the traffic is sufficiently light to enable you to stop virtually anywhere without causing a major traffic jam. A heron's eyesight is extremely keen, and though a hunting bird may well tolerate a vehicle driving past within a metre or so, the same animal will fly up in panic if a car stops too close by. The trick is to spot the bird as you are cruising around, but not to slow your pace of driving when you do so. Instead carry on, looking for suitable areas to bring the car round so that you may gain a clear view from the front passenger window or whichever port you have decided to use for photography or observation. When you are confident you have found this spot, drive at least 100 metres further before you turn to go back to it. Now is the time to prepare some sort of netting screen across the open window to cut down the heron's vision of your movements within. I use green scrim, both across the passenger window and the driver's side to help break up my outline. Now slowly drive back to the decided

waiting place and park the car quickly: too much moving backwards and forwards to get into position is likely to disturb the bird. Don't worry if the heron seems a long way off, just so long as you are reasonably close to the same water it is hunting on, the chances are the bird will eventually make its way towards you. If you attempt to take the car any closer than 50 metres or so, you will almost certainly frighten off your intended subject.

The other way to obtain good views of this species is to identify a favoured hunting place, set up a portable hide, and to wait. This can be very hit and miss, as most herons choose to feed over a wide variety of sites, rarely concentrating on one for any length of time. Exceptions occur when lakes or ditches are drained, exposing a glut of food, and such occasions are great for the observer.

Because herons usually build their nests in the tops of very tall trees, the only way to get good views without disturbing the colony is to build a scaffold nearby with a hide on top. As this species is generally quite faithful to a nesting site, the building is best done out of season, when the young birds have fledged, leaving the still obvious remains of a nesting platform. You run the risk of chilling and exposing the eggs to predators such as crows by erecting a scaffold when the adults are in the colony, particularly when they are incubating eggs.

My experiences of bitterns are limited to winter encounters, watching birds feeding on the edge of reed beds. All the best views have occurred in freezing conditions, forcing the bitterns out of the reeds in search of open water. They have always appeared to be nervy birds with excellent eyesight, and as such will demand the use of a hide for close views.

Most species in the heron family produce pellets of the undigested parts from their last meal, and these may be found at hunting sites or below nesting colonies. Most seem to end up in the water and so are lost, but I have found one or two on the banks of lakes and ditches which had been left by grey herons. These were all about five or so centimetres long, full of fish bones and scales, and rather ragged looking. Grey herons also leave distinctive footprints in soft mud and sand, the three spidery front toes and long hind toe spanning up to 10 centimetres.

Ducks

(Anatidae)

There are at least twenty-one species of duck breeding regularly in the British Isles, each of which displays its own idiosyncratic characteristics and habits.

There is no real trick to watching them, as most species of water birds make themselves obvious at some time or other. The reaction each displays to human presence varies enormously according to its experiences. Mallard, the most ubiquitous duck in the UK, can be so tame that it will take bread from your hand, or so timid that it will fly up at the first glimpse of an approaching person. Generally, though, all duck species are quite ready to accept a hide where necessary, and many can be closely observed without need of camouflage. This is especially true of many sea ducks: eider are particularly bold and may well not shift off the nest even when you are standing right next to them.

Many wetland reserves around the country have permanent hides built on prime sites and these can provide a first class view of many duck species. Failing this, the erection of a portable hide on a well used lake fringe can be equally rewarding. I have used floating hides from time to time (simply a portable hide built on a flat-bottomed boat) with reasonably good results, particularly on lakes and rivers which had dense bank vegetation.

When ducks are flying overhead, it is important that you either camouflage your face well, or avoid looking directly at them altogether, as many respond to the flash of a human face as a signal they are about to be shot at (often they are right).

Most ducks are ground nesters, with a few choosing to nest in tree hollows or other cavities. Some mallards nest in the bowls of trees or on rock ledges, and I have even seen one in a window box of a fifth storey apartment block. The chicks of all duck species leave the nest very soon after hatching and sometimes have to make monumental leaps from these inaccessible sites. Despite their fragile appearance, they are so light that even the most precipitous drop is handled with ease, their fluffy down absorbing all of the bumps and bangs of their first journey. The exodus of the nest usually occurs two or three days after hatching, and often first thing in the morning.

Many duck species fly by night and their flight calls can be a little confusing at first. The most unmistakable is the widgeon whose surprised whistle often heralds the arrival of the first frosts. Some species, notably mallard, widgeon and sometimes teal, can be drawn on to a body of water, particularly at dusk, by the careful placing of decoys and the use of artificial calls. Such methods have been tried and tested by many wildfowlers in pursuit of a bird or two for the pot, but the very same systems can be applied to benign observation.

Goose Species

(Anatidae)

Most of the geese which inhabit the British Isles do so through the winter months only. Having bred in the far north, they come to the relatively mild climate of the UK to graze on the salt marsh, bogland and fields of pasture, and many gather in huge flocks. The traditional feeding sites are well known and many are national reserves, providing permanent hides which afford clear views with no risk of disturbance.

Most truly wild geese are very nervous and will respond to the sight of a human form by taking instant, noisy flight. For really close views you need to identify fields which are being grazed and erect a hide within them. Such fields look cropped and trodden, with many large droppings scattered about. Simply plonking a hide bang smack in the middle of such a field is likely to frighten off the birds, and if they come down to graze at all, they will almost certainly be nervous of the structure. It is far better to try and site the hide close to an established shape, such as a gate or bush, and build it as low as possible, even digging a pit where you can (all this with the land owner's permission, of course).

Arrive at the hide well before first light and approach with care, particularly if there has been a full moon, as the birds may already be present and feeding. Prepare for a long wait, and at all costs avoid startling the geese. Though their eyesight is only good and not great, they are capable of spotting movement from a long range, and if one gets nervous (a wary bird cranes its neck and often bobs its head), the response is infectious, travelling through the flock in a matter of seconds.

The most common view of wild geese, and for me the most evocative, is to be had as they fly overhead on migration. Such a spectacle could be easily overlooked were it not for the birds' habit of calling almost continuously as they wend their way. Familiarity with these calls will ensure a great many more sightings during the autumn and spring. Nocturnal migration is common, and I have often stood outside on a chill October night, marvelling to the sound of white-fronted geese passing overhead.

Nesting birds will sit very tight, but may be reluctant to return if a hide is immediately placed close to the site. If you do locate a nest, move away instantly and only contemplate introducing a hide the next day, and even then starting at at least a range of 100 metres, moving in slowly over a period of days. The use of artificial decoys and calls may aid with calming birds down and convincing them that a field is safe to settle on.

All this applies only to geese which are truly wild. There are many geese which, though living wild, come originally from feral populations, most notably Canada geese. These can be very easy to observe and require no special preparation.

Swans

(Anatidae)

The most common swan in the UK is the mute, whose cousins, Bewick's and whooper swans are largely winter visitors.

Mute swans are perhaps one of the most accessible birds in the country, their large size and often bold manner making them ideal candidates for close study. They will tolerate very intimate observations at close range without the need for a hide in most cases. However, the use of a hide when watching close to a nest is well advised for your own protection as many male swans, or cobs as they are known, are very bold in defence of their mate and eggs. I have twice been 'beaten up' by these birds, and though my arm was not broken, I certainly knew I had been hit. When a swan walks up to you with its wings held high above its back and its head low, you should definitely consider moving away.

Certain aspects of swan posturing and calling help in predicting their movements. These can be particularly useful when photographing or filming. Birds that are about to take flight generally swim purposefully to one extreme edge of the body of water they are using, producing a thin, reedy call (a bit like someone whistling with grass) and holding their head and neck very high and erect. Courting birds often swim side by side to an open area of water before proceeding on their complex and very beautiful display of head shaking and neck dipping, which is a prelude to mating. Busking, as it is known, is the aggressive posture adopted by both the male and female swan either in response to other birds (whether they be swans or just a passing duck) invading the nesting territory, or towards any animal which is perceived as a threat. A busking swan holds its closed wing high over its back, producing a sail-like effect, and doubling the bird's profile, whilst tucking its head way back into its shoulders.

Busks are often followed up with charges where a bird, usually the male, makes a very noisy and intimidating clattering flight across the water in the direction of its intended target. If this display is not enough to scare off the intruder, it may well be followed up with a beating, where the swan uses the carpal joint of its wing to deliver very well aimed blows on to the body and head of the antagonist, whether it is a fox or a human being. Swans only attack after giving good warning, and my own beatings only came as a result of my ignoring these.

Though their name implies a complete lack of vocalization, this is not the case. Mute swans do not, however, respond dramatically to recordings of their calls, even those which are uttered in response to intruders to a territory. They show more interest in recordings of the whistle produced by the wing beats, perhaps the most distinctive and certainly the loudest sound made by the birds, but are not usually compelled to come close to its source and investigate.

Most Bewick's and whooper swans arrive in the UK for the winter, using coastal salt flats and areas of flat pasture for feeding. Where the birds are regularly feeding, similar techniques to those used with geese can be employed for close observation.

Birds of Prey

(Accipitridae)

Of all the birds in Europe, the raptors undoubtedly excite most interest. Their predatory lifestyle can provide some of the most spectacular of encounters in the field, from the effortless, sailing flights of the harriers to the exhilarating high speed stoops of a peregrine falcon.

Raptors (or bops as some bird watchers describe them, short for bird of prey) are fortunately quite visible creatures, often giving themselves away by the effect they have on every neighbouring bird and some mammals. This effect can vary from general alarm calls to direct mobbing, where other species actively pursue and heckle the raptor. The reason for the latter behaviour has been the subject of much debate, but appears to be a way of drawing attention to the danger, keeping it in view and hopefully dissuading it from staying in the area: it makes perfect sense to keep an eye on your enemy to avoid being taken by surprise. Each species of raptor has a different effect on the birds which are likely to react with alarm to it. Peregrine falcons elicit a dramatic response whereas kestrels may be ignored by many species. The alarm calls and predator response behaviour of each bird is different, though once learnt, can all lead to a massive increase in the number of bops you see in the field. These calls are distinct and varied (though often omitted from bird song recordings or identification guide texts) and every species of bird produces its own unique proclamation that danger is near. Many of these calls share a strident, siblant or metallic quality, which, even to the human ear, demand attention. Once familiar with the calls made by the more common birds, you will develop an ear for those made by others.

Blue tits and great tits are very common and very quick to respond to an airborne raptor. As both species feature high on the list of favourites for sparrowhawks, their anxiety is hardly surprising. Blue tits produce a very high-pitched, thin whistle which roughly follows the rhythm and notation of their song but lacks the body. The sound is very pure and piercing, best described as 'Tssss–Tssss–Tssss–ts–s–s–s–sst' where the staccato notes drop in pitch, then rise again at the end. Sometimes just one or two piercing whistles are uttered. Great tits will also utter a high-pitched whistle at the sight of a raptor flying overhead, but are generally more silent under these conditions than their cousins.

Starlings are another ubiquitous species which often play sentinel to both other birds and naturalists alike. Starling alarm is a short, metallic 'Psst', uttered either from the perch or in flight. Its volume and urgent sound demand attention, which is precisely what it is designed to do. In flight, starlings bunch into tight flocks, wheeling and twisting as one. This bunching is also a sure sign that a raptor is nearby, and can be seen from an incredible distance. Like all birds, starlings seem to be able to identify the species of bop which has caught their eye, and whereas a kestrel or buzzard will only produce one or two alarm calls and the most half-hearted and briefest of bunching flights, a sparrowhawk or peregrine will spark off a cacophony of calls and most vigorous and tightly packed flocking behaviour. This response relates directly to the

danger the raptor species represents to a starling. During the summer months, swallows and house martins are great early warning systems of an approaching bop. Swallows make a very metallic-sounding call at the sight of a raptor, particularly if they see a sparrowhawk or hobby. The

sound 'Pss-st ... Pss-st' has a ringing quality, like so many of the alarm calls, and is produced more or less frequently depending on the perceived severity of the threat.

House martins make a much more subdued alarm call, to our ears at least. Quite unlike their normal chattering flight calls, this hushed, descending trill is instantly echoed throughout a colony as soon as one bird emits it. It is normally produced in response only to bird hunting hawks, particularly hobbys, sparrowhawks and peregrines.

Blackbirds will produce a very thin, drawn-out whistle at the sight of an airborne raptor, but are far more noticeable when they find one hiding in cover. The 'Pink ... pink ... pink ... pink' call of a mobbing blackbird may reveal anything from a sleeping tawny owl to a crouching fox.

Virtually every species of passerine has a distinctive alarm call. By using these more common calls as a guide and listening to the less familiar ones which are stimulated at the same time, you can learn the language of fear which can make raptor spotting so much easier.

Quite apart from having such a dramatic, instant effect on their neighbours, birds of prey often leave other signs that they have been in an area. These come in the form of prey remains, droppings and pellets.

A raptor which has killed another bird invariably plucks it to some extent before feeding. Feathers which have been taken out by a hooked beak are usually intact right to the tip of the quill, unlike the frayed and chewed remains left by foxes and other mammalian predators. Some species, such as sparrowhawks, which specialize in bird hunting, may use a favourite spot for doing the job and these are known as plucking posts. These occur most often during the breeding season, when the male bird is returning regularly with prey to the same spot before preparing it for feeding. When not nesting, most kills are plucked very close to the point they are caught. Birds killed by bops may also display distinctive notches on their exposed breast bones which have been made by the beak of their executioner as it fed. With a bit of practice, and by taking into account prey size, species, habitat, injuries and general location, it is possible to make a pretty good stab at guessing the species of bop which has made a kill. This is not a precise science, however, and can only be a rough guide at best.

Most droppings from birds of prey are very white, sometimes creamy or pink, with little or no black content, and extremely liquid. The effect of repeated defecation in the same spot can be a dramatic whitewashing of all adjacent objects below. These white scars may betray both roosting, and late in the season, nesting sites of a number of species, especially the larger ones, such as buzzards and eagles. All raptors eject their guano forcibly, an adaptation which helps keep nestbound young from fouling their nursery, and the result is usually a wide scattering of the white remains below a single point.

All birds of prey cough up pellets of undigested food remains from time to time, and these, too, can give a clue to their whereabouts. These are only really useful as a guide to roosting sites where the pellets may build up in number, or to favoured hunting perches which may also sport a fair litter below. You rarely find many, if any, pellets below nests. Each species produces pellets which relate to its body size and prey items. Very few are as well rounded and torpedo-shaped as those produced by owls.

Watching bops is often something of a chance activity. Their wide-ranging habits and fast flight means that most views are brief and occur more by luck than judgment. There are times when and places where you can increase your chances of a sighting—for example, many raptors move out to the coast for the winter, and a day spent at an estuary or salt marsh in January may well provide views of several species, including hen harrier, merlin and peregrine. In summer the migrant species, such as hobby and honey buzzard, visit Europe to breed. Hobbys are most conspicuous as they hawk for dragonflies over southern wetlands, and honey buzzards, though skulking and elusive for most of the season, may be seen performing their acrobatic display flights early in the spring soon after they arrive from Africa. There are one or two bop migration hot-spots around Europe, where, quite literally, thousands of raptors of all types gather before making the flight across the sea to North Africa. Unfortunately, there is nowhere like this in the UK.

Some species will respond moderately to recordings of their calls, most notably buzzard, sparrowhawk and kestrel.

Many species of bop enjoy the full protection of the law, and as such must not be disturbed at the nest without a licence. Quite apart from protecting the remaining number of many species, this law helps to guard against unnecessary disturbance of what may well be a very nervous bird. Even the most common species, such as buzzard, are very highly strung, and may well abandon eggs or small young if they feel threatened. I have filmed many species of raptor nesting and have always treated them with the greatest of respect.

Many choose to nest in high, inaccessible places where the only method of getting a good view is to build a scaffolding tower with a hide on top nearby. Such a structure should, where possible, be built

only once the chicks have hatched and are of a size that ensures they can remain unbrooded for a while without suffering. Even then, all work at the site, which is likely to keep the adult birds away, must be limited to fifteen or twenty minute sessions, with several hours wait in between. Where it is necessary to build a hide during incubation of eggs or before, extreme care must be taken, keeping all exposed visits to an absolute minimum. Once in the hide for observation, remain there for a full day and use a walk-away to avoid suspicion.

All raptors have excellent eyesight, and this must be taken into account, even when using a hide. I usually wear full camouflage clothing, including face paint, as well as double the amount of usual netting over all open ports, to avoid making the birds nervous. Even then, it is sometimes obvious that a raptor has spotted a movement from a lens or within the hide, and if this occurs, a lengthy period of zero activity should be adopted before attempting to move again.

Despite the nervous disposition of some raptors, many will adapt quite quickly to a hide and the presence of a lens poking at them, and in time, so long as no adverse experiences occur, will become quite bold. I have even had a merlin regularly using the hide as a plucking post.

Partridge and Grouse Family

(Tetraonidae)

These chunky, ground-nesting birds are generally quite nervous because, as their commonly used generic name suggests, they are frequently shot for sport and the pot. Game birds range from the tiny quail to the spectacular capercaillie, and are frequently encouraged and managed to some extent for shooting interests.

The most ubiquitous species is undoubtedly the pheasant, which is commonly reared in hatcheries and released into managed woodlands and estates. Many of these released birds avoid the guns and manage to lead a feral existence.

Partridges, both the indigenous grey and the introduced red-legged, are fairly common around the country, more so where they are being actively encouraged for a shoot. They are both fairly nervous birds but can be watched with some ease by using a vehicle as a hide in suitably open habitats such as downland.

Black grouse, the males of which are spectacularly plumaged, are birds of moorland and birch woodland, and the best time and place for watching them is undoubtedly during the lek (when the birds congregate, fight and display for the attention of a female) in spring and early summer. Lekking sites are traditional and may be used by generations of birds. Areas of open heath or large clearings in wooded country are visited just on first light by many males who all start calling and displaying. By sun-up, the lek is in full swing and females are visiting to make their choice of suitor. Black grouse will readily accept a hide next to a lek so long as it has been gently introduced over a period of three or four days.

Both black and red grouse are usually spotted only as they 'flush' in front of a dog or human. In areas where they are very common, and before the shooting season has begun, it may be possible to get very close to feeding birds by using a vehicle as a hide. Erecting a portable hide simply to watch feeding behaviour may well be futile because the birds are wide-ranging and most of the habitats they frequent afford complete cover unless they are very close.

Ptarmigan are often more readily observed, particularly on snow covered hillsides, where groups of birds may be spotted at some distance, and a hide erected during the evening or night ready for the following day's activity. It is also possible to stalk this species using available cover, and with reasonable care you can get some very good views in this way.

Capercaillie are huge birds, but despite their size, can be very good at remaining invisible. Lekking sites can be identified by the calls of the male and trampled ground in suitable habitat. A hide can then be erected carefully on the edge of the site during the latter part of the day ready for a dawn start.

Most game birds leave large, distinctive droppings, particularly grouse, whose cylindrical, crumbly guano is often obvious among the heather.

Rails and Crakes

(Rallidae)

These are mainly birds of watery habitat with the exception of the corncrake which nests in open fields. Some of the family, moorhens and coots, are very easy to observe, particularly where they are used to human activity. Others, like the water rail, live a very secretive existence, creeping around in the cover of reed beds and the like. The best time for watching these more elusive birds is midwinter, when cover is low and ice forces them out into the open in search of food. At all times of year, water rails can make their presence known by emitting pig-like squeals and screeches from deep within cover. When they do show themselves they will often tolerate quite close observation so long as you remain still and quiet.

All are tolerant of a hide with no need for a lengthy introduction, and birds which nest on water regularly visited by people, such as park ponds, are very hardy and indifferent to most disturbance. My experiences with corncrake are limited to listening to their nocturnal calls and one glimpse of a bird which I inadvertently flushed from long grass. In areas where they still breed regularly, they are reputed to be quite tolerant of human activity, often nesting close to farm buildings.

Waders

(Haematopodidae to Scolopacidae)

There are forty or so species of wading bird which regularly visit the UK. Some are resident and breed; others visit only during the winter months to feed on the invertebrate-rich mud flats around the coastline. Indeed, many of the species which do breed here have their numbers boosted during the colder months by others of their kind moving down from the north of Europe. Most are ground nesting birds, and all, with the notable exception of the woodcock, are birds of open country, usually containing areas with plenty of damp ground.

Each species is unique in character; some are very hardy and accept any observation with little fuss. Others are incredibly nervous and must be treated with extreme caution around the nest site. Where the birds are feeding, it is often possible to erect a hide either on the feeding grounds, or, on the coast, at a roosting location which may be used at high tide. When waders are roosting, they are very vulnerable to predation, and as such are often very nervous. If you do any observation from a hide at a roosting site it is imperative that you remain within, before and during their arrival, and up until the last bird leaves the roost.

As is the case with so many ground-nesting birds, extreme care must be taken to avoid disturbance when attempting to use a hide close to a nest. This usually entails a very gradual introduction after discovery of the nest, starting with the hide at least 200 or 300 metres away for most species, and only moving it in when you are confident the bird has settled back on the nest with no qualms whatsoever.

Many wading birds indulge in complex displays, often involving high flying and stylized calling. The best known and most spectacular are the whiffling flights of lapwing, the plunge diving of drumming snipe and the parachute descents of curlew. All these draw attention to the general area which may be chosen for nesting.

Watching waders feeding on tidal mud flats or mussel beds can be a challenge due to the constant movement of water. This makes the erection of a hide difficult. The simple answer is to use a floating hide— a boat which is anchored in place with a hide on top—which settles on to the feeding grounds as the tide drops, leaving you in the perfect position for very close views. It pays to leave such a structure in position for several days before you attempt a stake-out, to allow birds using the area to acclimatize to it.

Woodcock are somewhat different from all their cousins because they prefer damp woodland as a feeding and nesting habitat. Most views occur by accident as you frighten a bird from cover, but during spring and summer it is possible to watch the display flights of the male bird, known as roding, which takes place at dusk. In this display the bird flies on stiff wings just above the tree level, constantly uttering a strange croaking and whistling call. If you do catch sight of this display, hang around even after the bird has disappeared, because the flight is made in circuits around the territory and in a few minutes it will almost certainly come past again.

Another species, which is allied to the waders but generally prefers a drier habitat, is the stone curlew. These birds of open farmland and downland can be remarkably inconspicuous, spending much of the day crouching low to the ground asleep. In the early morning and evening, they may put on a show of calling and displaying to secure a mate and territory, and this activity may extend into the darkness. In an area where several pairs are breeding in close proximity, observation from a hide placed equidistant between two territories should provide good views of this sort of behaviour. The nest itself should be treated with caution, only slowly introducing a hide from a distance, and remaining very still within it due to the bird's excellent eyesight.

Most waders have keen sight and will respond adversely to movement. This ability makes them great sentinels for an approaching bird of prey, and many, such as dunlin and knot, form great swirling flocks when a raptor is nearby.

Skuas and Gulls

(Stercorariidae, Laridae)

All of these birds adapt quickly to the introduction of a hide at any stage of the nesting period. When filming a herring gull colony, there were many occasions when the birds used the hide as a perch and I even had young birds trying to come inside. They were not put off, even when I waggled my finger at them from beneath the canvas, in fact they just pecked me.

Skuas can be very bold at the nest, and many of the larger gulls share the skua's habit of attacking any intruder by diving from the air and striking with their feet. Such attacks can draw blood from an unwary human head.

Outside the nesting period, many of these birds spend a great deal of time at sea, and can be watched using the same sea spotting techniques described in the section Petrels, Shearwaters and Fulmar. Some of the best views are to be had as the birds follow fishing trawlers, picking up the scraps thrown overboard.

A challenging way to watch for the rarer gull species is to visit a roosting site. On large bodies of inland fresh water, these communal roosts may often contain many thousands of birds which stream in from all directions, often flying high and direct to the centre of the lake, where they whiffle erratically down to the surface for a bath and a sleep. Picking out the only Mediterranean gull from a flock of 400 black-headed gulls is like trying to find a needle in a haystack. And of course, there is no guarantee that the flocks contain any rarer species at all. Whether your interest is in rarities or just enjoying the spectacle of thousands of birds collecting against a reddening sky, a visit to a gull roost is always good value.

Terns

(Sternidae)

All terns visit the UK only in the summer, and the first arrivals are as much a sign of the season as any swallow. Indeed, this trait and their general outline of forked tail and swept back wings has earned them the name 'sea swallows'.

Most nest in colonies of anything from a handful of pairs to many hundreds. Because they breed on the ground, they are very vulnerable to the effects of high tides and storms, as well as predation from gulls, crows, foxes, mink and otters. Despite this, they are vigorous defenders of a nesting site, and any person entering a colony of common terns is likely to suffer repeated attacks from their needle-sharp beaks. By disturbing the birds from the nest, you increase the chances of predation and risk stepping on the well camouflaged eggs. All terns that I have filmed readily accept a hide built in their midst, though, where possible, this is best done before they return to a favoured site in the spring. They take little notice of careful if any movement within the hide.

Terns generally hunt over open water, seeking small fish and other animals. As such, their hunting behaviour is fairly hard to predict, though where pickings are rich reasonably close to a nesting colony, many birds will choose to hunt, particularly once the chicks have hatched.

Common, arctic and little terns will also follow some human fishing activities, such as long netting for whitebait, and will pick off the fish that escape the nets. This can provide the observer with some excellent views in a predictable spot. Birds hunting in this manner take little notice of a person nearby.

Auks

(Alcidae)

These include razorbills, guillemots, little auks and puffins. All but the little auk breed in the UK, either on sea cliffs or in holes and crevices nearby. Puffins choose to nest underground, often in disused rabbit warrens or manx shearwater burrows. Many puffin colonies are well known and sited on nature reserves. These are often very easy to watch, without need of a hide, as the adult birds fly in and out of the nest holes with beaks full of sand eels. The other auks, particularly razorbills and guillemots, are much more nervous, and if you do find a site which allows close observation, the use of a hide is a good idea.

Birds feeding at sea do so randomly, following shoals of small fish, often some way from shore in the summer, and well out to sea in the winter months. Getting close views of this hunting behaviour is not easy, as the birds do not like being approached too closely by a boat. Use of a scope from a promontory or headland which is frequented by the birds often provides the best views.

Pigeons and Doves

(Columbidae)

All pigeons and doves respond well to hides, though where shot at regularly, you may need to use a decoy placed close to the feeding or roosting area you are watching to convince some species that the coast is clear.

Woodpigeons roost communally through the winter, and the ground below such a site is covered with their droppings. These have a musty scent and frequently contain the seeds of ivy berries or grain. When woodpigeons take flight, they do so with a noisy clatter of wings, letting every living thing in the vicinity know that danger is near.

Other species, such as collard doves and feral pigeons, are so well adapted to a life with man that no special techniques are required for observation, except the respect you would employ working with any animal.

Owls

(Tytonidae, Strigidae)

One of the most popular of bird families, owls have captured the imagination for many generations. In the UK there are three fairly common species and three others of varying degrees of rarity. All are nocturnal or crepuscular, though little owls, short-eared, and barn owls may all remain active during daylight, particularly when raising a family.

One of the most successful ways of getting a good view of the more nocturnal species, such as tawny owl, is to mimic their call or use a recording of the same. This technique works best when the birds are establishing territories: March and October are good months for tawny owl song, November and February or March for long-eared owls. Both of these species usually spend the day roosting in dense undergrowth, and only start to venture out as the light is fading.

Finding the birds as they sleep can be very difficult, because they are both well camouflaged and may remain motionless even when you are just a few metres away, but there are a few signs which may help locate them. One is the litter of pellets and sometimes droppings that they leave beneath a favoured roosting site. Long-eared owl pellets are a little smaller than those of the tawny owl, which, at about 5 cm long, are a full centimetre bigger. Both are elongated and usually comprise grey masses of fur surrounding a collection of small bones from prey items.

Pellet peeling can be great fun, and reveal a great deal about the diet of the birds which produce them. Droppings of both species are usually creamy-white and often lack any black content. Roosting owls are frequently the subject of intense mobbing behaviour from a variety of other birds and even squirrels. Calls produced by these creatures are typical of finding a static or perched danger, the most far-reaching and ubiquitous being that of the blackbird. Other species which get very excited and vociferous if they find a sleeping owl include jay, chaffinch, song thrush, blue and great tits, and mistle thrush. Many of these birds feature in the diet of both types of owl and so have good reason to be a little nervous of one sleeping in their midst.

Tawny owls use cavities in trees as nesting sites, often with a vertical approach hole. You should be very careful indeed when checking potential nest sites, because the adult birds can be aggressive in defence of their eggs and young striking out at a human face with their talons. Long-eared owls use old crows' nests or similar structures as a place to rear a family, and are much less aggressive than tawnys.

Little owls will respond well to a mimicked call and quickly come to investigate its source. That they are active by day, especially at dawn and dusk, is of enormous benefit to the observer, and to achieve really close and prolonged views, the use of a hide is usually essential. This species does most of its hunting from low perches, picking off anything from earthworms to small mammals and birds. I have successfully used the car as a hide to watch this sort of behaviour.

Eggs are usually laid in a tree cavity, though one year we had little owls nesting under the tiles of our roof. As the chicks develop, they frequently venture out of the nest chamber long before they are able to fly and clamber around the branches. I have found that you can usually confirm a suspected nest site late in the season by mimicking the call of an adult owl. If well grown chicks are within the cavity, they will almost certainly become excited and start their wheezy call notes, perhaps even poking their heads out to see who's coming. Little owl pellets are small, about 3 cm or so, and usually blunt ended (kestrel pellets, which are about the same size, usually have a tapered end).

Barn owls respond to mimicked and recorded calls, though particularly during the period when they are quartering their territories early in the year, usually from January to June.

Across much of their transglobal range, barn owls are strictly nocturnal birds, only venturing out half an hour or so after sunset and settling to roost well before dawn. In the UK, however, they can be surprisingly diurnal, more so when feeding a young family or when weather conditions have prevented hunting during the night. The spectacle of this ghost-like bird floating low over the ground on silent wings make it one of the natural treasures of the British countryside.

Much of the filming and observation I have done of this species hunting has been from a vehicle, driving around suitable, flat habitat until I spot a flying bird, then pulling over to watch it. When doing this, it is important to be aware of wind direction, not because the owl will smell you—no worries there—but more to provide you with a good head-on view of the flying bird. A barn owl, like virtually any other bird, will fly into the wind out of preference when hunting to ensure as slow a ground speed as possible. They will even hover from time to time. By positioning yourself upwind of a hunting bird, you stand a far greater chance of having it fly straight towards you than if you had the wind in your face.

When you are familiar with the movements of an individual barn owl, it is sometimes possible to predict which fields it is likely to use during the course of its evening or dawn hunting sessions, and set up well in advance of the bird's arrival. You can achieve some incredibly close views in this manner, particularly if you crouch low in long grass or other available cover.

As their name suggests, barn owls frequently nest on ledges in old farm buildings, but will also use hollow trees and small rocky caves. In Africa they regularly use large holes in sand banks, often the result of several bee-eater tunnels collapsing into one. Where a barn owl roosts, it leaves a litter of pellets below. These are much rounder than other owl pellets and usually have a glossy black sheen on the exterior surface. Each pellet measures roughly 5 cm in length.

Activity at the nest may start a good two hours before sunset in summer, with the male doing the lion's share of the hunting. This species can be quite accommodating at the nest site, readily accepting a hide which is built nearby. Care must be taken not to disturb the birds in the middle of the day when they are incubating eggs, because repeated flushing of the brooding female may cause her to desert.

Once a hide is in place and accepted, you must be careful not to make loud or sudden noises, as, unusually among birds, owls react negatively to sound as a consequence of their extremely sensitive and directional hearing. Their excellent eyesight also dictates that great care must be taken to avoid sudden movement within the hide.

Of the other species of owl likely to be seen in the UK, the short-eared owl is the most abundant and obvious, often hunting in broad daylight during the winter, sometimes in quite large numbers. I have seen up to fifteen hunting along a single stretch of coastal marsh in some years, usually when the populations of vole are at their highest. Short-eared owls can be treated in much the same way as a hunting barn owl, paying special attention to wind direction for the best views. I have also 'squeaked' them to within a few yards, by lying in long grass close to a hunting bird and making a sound like a mouse. The inquisitive birds often circle or clumsily hover directly overhead for several seconds before moving on.

Nightjars

(Caprimulgidae)

These wholly nocturnal birds are a disappearing feature of many British heaths and forests, a great pity because their churring song and wavering flight seem to me as much a part of a British summer on heathland as gorse flower.

The first birds arrive in the country from their African winter in mid-spring, and the males immediately start setting up territory. The wing-clapping display flights and 'fishing-reel' song punctuate the coming of night, as the birds argue over choice nesting sites.

Nightjar watching is best done in midsummer when the evenings are at their longest and the birds are still vociferous. The male and female will respond strongly to recordings, but I have never been able successfully to mimic their calls by mouth convincingly. They are quite bold in their scrutiny of unknown voices, and will flap around your head under the right conditions.

Nests are nothing more than a scrape on the ground, and though the female will sit very tight during the day, her magnificent camouflage rendering her virtually invisible, the same bird can be quite nervous at night around the nest. I have virtually stood on an unseen bird whilst it was incubating eggs in daylight, but found the same nightjar to be intolerant of a hide which I introduced the next evening 6 metres away. I moved from the site after twenty minutes of being watched by an anxious parent and made a much more gradual and successful approach over a period of several days.

Nightjars will accept artificial light at the nest so long as it is introduced gradually from a dim glow upwards.

Kingfishers

(Alcedinidae)

If you are just getting into bird watching, you almost certainly want to see a kingfisher, and even if you have seen them hundreds of times it is impossible to tire of their magnificent plumage and jaunty character.

When first trying to catch a glimpse of this little jewel, it can be terribly frustrating attempting to keep your eyes fixed on a stretch of river in an attempt to spot the flash of azure blue as it belts by at a rate of knots. All too often it slips past before you know it and has disappeared around a bend in the stream. But spotting kingfishers is really quite easy once you know their call, because a flying bird almost continuously whistles, warning other kingfishers in the stream of its approach, and aiding the naturalist in his or her quest. A kingfisher whistle is a strident single or double note that really does catch the ear once it is familiar. It most closely resembles the call note of a dunnock, but is much more strident and sibilant. (You may not believe this, but as I wrote that last sentence, a kingfisher flew up the river past my office window, calling as it went . . . Spooky eh?!)

Where the birds perch to hunt, they leave a spattering of very white droppings. You may also find the odd tiny pellet of undigested fish bones.

Having established that a kingfisher is using a stretch of water, it is very easy to set up a hide next to a favoured perch, because the birds take little or no notice of a new structure arriving overnight, despite being very nervous of an exposed human form. In fact, it is often possible to provide the kingfisher with a new perch over a fishing site.

Look for a pale, horizontal branch which will overhang the water by at least a metre and is a metre above the surface. Drive this into the bank where no other perches exist for several metres either side and set up a hide nearby. It is amazing how quickly the kingfishers may try out this new vantage point, and if you have done your job well, it may well turn into the bird's favourite fishing place.

Kingfishers nest in tunnels dug into the vertical face of a waterside bank, and so remain hidden as they incubate and feed their young. It is possible to dig an observation port into the nest chamber, replacing the soil with a small plate of glass. Such an intrusion is potentially stressful for the birds unless handled very carefully, and should only be attempted with very good reason.

When working with tunnel nesters, I generally dig a large pit alongside which will house me and all my equipment. I ensure this pit can be made entirely light-proof. I then gently chisel into the side of the chamber, at first only exposing a centimetre or so, then replace this section with a small piece of glass, put dark fabric over the back and leave. In slow and gentle stages this hole is enlarged, and other ports for fibre optic lighting are introduced. As always, if at any stage the adult seems nervous, the project is abandoned and the nest rebuilt. That said, I have never experienced any problems with kingfishers, and all the nests I have worked with have successfully reared young.

Where observation or photography of a nest exterior is wanted, the careful introduction of a suitable perch, either just below or in the bank nearby, will provide the birds with a handy resting point and you with an ideal view of a perched kingfisher.

Woodpeckers
(Picidae)

These colourful birds are often overlooked due to their arboreal habits and skulking, almost mammal-like movements through the tree tops.

The most common and easiest to watch is the great spotted woodpecker, which is as likely to visit a suburban garden as be seen in a deciduous woodland. In early spring, both the male and female proclaim territorial rights by drumming on the resonant branch of a tree. Though this drumming is quite hard to mimic (the birds produce eight or so beats a second, not easy to do with your hand), you can attract the attention of an inquisitive woodpecker by reproducing the sounds made by a feeding bird. By holding a small stone and sporadically tapping a dead branch or hollow tree in the manner of a bird searching for grubs beneath the bark, you may well be the subject of interest from the local woodpeckers, particularly during the spring and summer. Do not overdo the tapping, leave good long gaps between bouts or you will quickly bore the birds and they will disappear. Equally, once you have had a reasonable view, stop the tapping and allow the woodpeckers to go about their business. Though there is nothing to suggest that use of this sort of trick has the slightest detrimental effect on the birds, I always feel that such a technique should be kept to a minimum, out of good manners if nothing else.

Great spotted woodpeckers often visit gardens in winter to feed on nut bags or other tit-bits that are left out. A favourite woodpecker snack is a bit of animal fat, and this is best proffered in a purpose-built woodpecker feeder. Find a suitably rough barked branch or stump and drill many centimetre holes up its length. Then drive this into the ground and fill the holes with fat. As well as catering for woodpeckers, this system is one of the few which will be used regularly by tree creepers, a bird which normally misses out on the bounty from a bird table due to its very specific feeding requirements.

When a woodpecker is preparing a nest hollow in a tree, it is often made obvious by the copious litter of wood chips below. Great spotted woodpeckers are very comfortable with a hide nearby or even a careful and motionless observer waiting outside the nest, but care must be taken not to interrupt the bird's usual flight path to and from the site, if the use of a scaffold is considered for a better view. It is also possible to prepare a nest hollow for internal observation by carefully chiselling one wall away and replacing it with glass, preventing light and movement from being seen by the nesting birds with the use of a hide and a quantity of black fabric.

Lesser spotted woodpeckers are a much less conspicuous bird, generally keeping to the tree tops and rarely feeding on any food which is offered during winter. I have managed once or twice to attract a territorial male by mimicking feeding taps on a branch, but rarely with as much success as can be had with great spotted woodpeckers.

Green woodpeckers are one of the most colourful birds in Europe, though this splendour is often lost because their vivid green plumage blends in so well with the grass they so frequently hunt on. The main diet of this species is ants and their larvae which are dragged from their underground nests by the long sticky tongue of the woodpecker.

Of all the woodpecker species in the UK, green woodpeckers are generally the most nervous, though this does not prevent them from often showing up on well-manicured lawns in suburban gardens. Where they feed regularly, it is possible to set up a hide for close observation. This will be readily accepted so long as no obvious or sudden moves are made within. Use any available existing cover to help break up the outline of the hide and try to station it close to a stock of ants' nests. Take care here, though; I once spent the day filming a woodpecker feeding on the ant-infested lawn of a cottage garden, only to find that later the same evening, I had also been infested, and nursed incredibly itchy legs for the next few days.

Green woodpeckers are comfortable with a hide within 5 metres or so of the exterior of the nest, but are very nervous of any internal disturbance. Among the most vocal of its family, this species will respond to a recording of the laughing call which has earned the bird its country name of yaffle.

The Passerines

(Alaudidae to Emberizidae)

The passerines or perching birds include a wide variety of species, from the familiar blackbird and sparrow, to nightingales and orioles. Each species has its own set of field signs and behavioural quirks, though to deal with each individually would fill a whole book alone.

Many species are sufficiently similar to lump together under one heading. Many leave no field signs whatsoever, and you must rely on a sound knowledge of song and markings to find and identify them.

Larks and Pipits

(Alaudidae, Motacillidae)

These birds are generally great songsters. Their display flights are designed to attract attention, and as such are the best clue for locating them. In common with almost all small passerines, they completely ignore the introduction of a hide close to the nest so long as care is taken not to block the usual approach routes of the adult birds. Those which use a song post, such as tree pipits, may do so regularly enough for you to set up a hide nearby to achieve closer views.

Martins and Swallows

(Hirundinidae)

All these birds are exclusively summer migrants to the UK. They are very hardy and readily accept a hide or even an exposed observer near the nest site. The often inaccessible nature of the nests may require the use of scaffolding for close views and this is also virtually ignored by the birds.

Swallows and house martins both use damp mud in the construction of their nests, and if the early part of the year has been dry, such building material may be hard to come by. Creating an artificial damp mud patch at times like these will always attract these birds if they are nesting nearby. Simply by allowing a hose to run onto a bare patch of soil, away from any bushes or other cover which may be concealing a cat or other danger, will be sufficient to tempt most down for a squishy beakful.

Sand martins are tunnel nesters, returning year after year to well established colony sites. In common with their cousins, they are very obliging with close observation, though use of a hide is usually necessary for very intimate views.

Crows

(Corvidae)

The crows are generally relatively intelligent, nervous birds, with excellent eyesight. There are no special techniques used in watching crows other than taking the same sort of precautions needed for a bird of prey to avoid disturbing them. This applies particularly to any observations made at the nest, as some corvids, carrion crows, ravens and jays more than others, can be very nervy.

If scaffolding is to be used for nest observation, it should be built in short bursts, over a period of several days, with a constant check on the response of the returning adults. Any movement from binoculars or lenses in the hide window will frighten the birds unless they have become completely accustomed to its presence. Members of the crow family which include carrion in their diet can be attracted close to a hide by putting out a carcass nearby.

The Tit Family

(Paridae)

Some of the most common garden birds are included in this group, and as such they provide the naturalist with a fascinating insight to bird behaviour without having to stray past the front door. The use of nuts to attract great tits and blue tits into the garden during the winter months is no secret. In fact, looking at the incredible array of exotic bird-feeders available on the market, it is very big business. So too is the sale of bird nesting boxes, many of which are designed specifically for these birds.

It is perfectly straightforward to build a simple nest box; any number of books and publications have the details, or failing this, a quick call to your local conservation body should put you right. Very few are designed for interior observation, however, and though this may sound like a terrible intrusion into the bird's private life, if carefully done it causes little or no stress, and can provide some extraordinary and intimate views of an otherwise hidden episode of these common birds' lives.

I usually make boxes from natural materials, a hollow log, for example, but if the look of the interior is not important, any standard nest box design will do. The major difference is that the back is missing to provide a view of the interior. The most important part of establishing this sort of nest box is the location, which must be on a shed wall or equivalent that can have a hole cut in it and provide a dry, dark space for you to sit and watch in. Before putting the nest box up, prepare two frames, one on the exterior of the shed wall into which the box will slot and so provide a dry, draught free seal, and another on the inside of the shed which can receive the various backs. These should also be prepared before you set the box on the wall, and should include a plain solid back that will remain in place until such time as a bird sets up residence, a glass back of the same dimensions which can be slotted in for viewing purposes, and possibly one with fabric stretched across a frame for sound recording. The hole is then cut in the shed wall, the box attached, the solid back put in place and fingers crossed that a bird will like it!

Though very careful observations can be undertaken right from the nest building stage, it is far better to wait until the eggs have hatched and the chicks are at least a week old before starting any exchange of solid back for the glass one. So long as the interior of the shed is completely dark, you wear subdued clothing and face covering, and refrain from too much movement, the adult birds should continue feeding as though nothing had happened once the glass is in place. Sometimes they may seem a little surprised at the first visit back after the exchange, but assuming you are not visible, this is usually due to them spotting their own reflections in the glass. If you cannot provide a light-proof seal, it is often a good idea to pin a sheet of black felt across the back of the glass with a tiny hole cut in it for observation. This doubly ensures no shocking view of a human being in the back of the nest appears before the parent birds. When you have concluded observations for the day, wait for the parent birds to leave the nest, get an assistant to stand outside to prevent their premature re-entry, and replace the solid wooden back, both for warmth and to ensure no accidental exposure to the open back occurs in your absence.

This system can be used for a wide range of hole-nesting birds, but it demands extreme care at all times.

Dipper, Dunnock and other LBJs

This section covers the remaining species of birds most common in Britain. LBJs refer to 'little brown jobs'. It includes some which have very specific habits and watching methods, such as dippers and nightingales, and many others which fall into the category where the only tip for watching them is to go into the field with binoculars and look around.

Many of these birds will respond to a recording of their song, and for skulking species such as nightingale and cuckoo, this can be one of the only ways to ensure a good view. This method of observation must be used with great restraint when birds are nesting, as a bird investigating your recording is neglecting other pressing duties such as feeding. That said, I have found many birds will become bored with, or wise to, the trickery in a short time, ignoring all other attempts to entice them into the open with song. For both reasons, I generally keep all observations done in this way of an individual bird to ten or fifteen minutes a day, spread over a period of several hours.

The dipper is unusual in that it keeps almost exclusively to a life on fast-flowing rivers and streams. The pure white, very waxy droppings on rocks in the middle of such waters are a sure sign that dippers are present. Like kingfishers, this species could easily be missed as it dashes past on whirring wings were it not for the flight call which is regularly uttered as the bird flits from place to place. This little zipping tweet is surprisingly piercing over the sound of rushing water and almost always pre-empts the arrival of the bird into view. The same call is often uttered as the dipper perches on a rock or log between bouts of diving.

This species is very tolerant of hides, both at the nest and close to feeding locations.

Very few of the remaining species of bird leave any characteristic signs or require complicated methods in field craft for observing them. Most are very tolerant of hides at the nest, and many are very trusting even with an exposed human being nearby. A notable exception is the crossbill, whose habit of splitting open fir cones to reach the seeds, leaves characteristically shattered remains, with each scale of the cone split from top to bottom.

For the other species, the only way I have found to achieve prolonged and predictable views of most is to entice them with food. This may range from a liberal scattering of rotting apples for redwing and fieldfare, to a sprinkling of poppy seeds in the head of a teasel to encourage goldfinches and linnets.

Many birds will use a shallow pool of water for drinking and bathing, and a purpose-built pool in an otherwise dry woodland may well provide some superb views.

The methods used for observing wildlife do not end with this book—far from it. For every species there is a peculiar approach, a system and a sympathy which apply to that creature alone and indeed frequently to the individual you are observing. Every invertebrate, amphibian and insect displays unique traits of behaviour which must be accommodated if you are successfully to observe it in a stress-free environment, and discovering these methods is very much a part of the thrill of wildlife observation.

If you follow some of the techniques I have covered in this book you will ensure your subjects suffer the minimum of disturbance, whilst at the same time enjoy the unfolding of a world which to a great many people will remain hidden forever.

With your developing knowledge, you will undoubtedly come to respect and care for wild things which I hope will inspire you to help protect these precious and vulnerable treasures.

Index

Numerals in bold face indicate a chapter/section devoted to a subject entry. Simon King is referred to as SK throughout the index.